MARY JANE WALKER

Mary Jane Walker is a writer of well-informed travel narratives that come with a historical flavour.

Living in the Southern Hemisphere, Mary Jane was long fascinated by the lands at the other end of her world. *Incredible Iceland* is her latest book, the result of her long-held ambition to visit the island nation that does, indeed, take its name from the ice with which it is partly covered.

With many pictures, maps, and links to illustrated blog posts and videos, *Incredible Iceland* is a great introduction to a fascinating nation!

For her previous works, Mary Jane has won a bronze medal from IPPY (the Independent Publisher Book Awards) for *The Neglected North Island* (2020) and was placed, before that, as a finalist in travel in two other competitions for *A Maverick New Zealand Way* and *Iran: Make Love Not War*.

Email: maryjanewalker@a-maverick.com
Facebook: facebook.com/amavericktraveller
Instagram: @a_maverick_traveller
Linkedin: Mary Jane Walker
Pinterest: amavericktraveller
TikTok: @amavericktraveller1
Twitter: @Mavericktravel0

a-maverick.com

Published 2021 by Mary Jane Walker

A Maverick Traveller Ltd

PO Box 44 146, Point Chevalier, Auckland 1246

NEW ZEALAND

a-maverick.com

ISBN-13:

978-0-473-58982-0 (softcover POD)

978-0-473-58984-4 (mobi)

978-0-473-58983-7 (epub)

978-0-473-58985-1 (digital audiobook).

Disclaimer

This book is a travel memoir, not an outdoors guide. Although the author and publisher have made every effort to ensure that the information in this book was correct at the time of publication, the author and publisher do not assume and hereby disclaim any liability to any party for any loss, damage, or disruption caused by errors or omissions, whether such errors or omissions result from negligence, accident, or any other cause. Some names have also been changed to disguise and protect certain individuals.

Covers and Fonts

Front cover and spine fonts are Impact Condensed. The interior text is typeset primarily in Garamond, with image captions mainly in Times New Roman.

A Note on Maps and Images

IF you have a copy of this book in which the images are printed in black and white, or if you have a reader with a black-and-white screen, you can see all of the images in this book that were originally in colour in full colour, and all of the images including chapter-specific maps generally at higher resolution, by going to the blog posts linked at the end of each chapter.

In fact, these blog posts may contain more images and other visual material than appears in the book.

Unless noted or indicated otherwise, all maps, aerial photos and satellite images are shown with north at the top.

Readers are in every case urged to make use of original maps (often zoomable if online) and guides when in the outdoors; the maps and aerial/satellite images shown in this book are purely for illustration.

For a literally more all-round perspective, you might also wish to look at some of localities I describe in the 3D view on Google Earth.

Lastly, all maps and other images in the book and related blog posts are the property of Mary Jane Walker unless otherwise credited.

Contents

Front Matter

Introduction

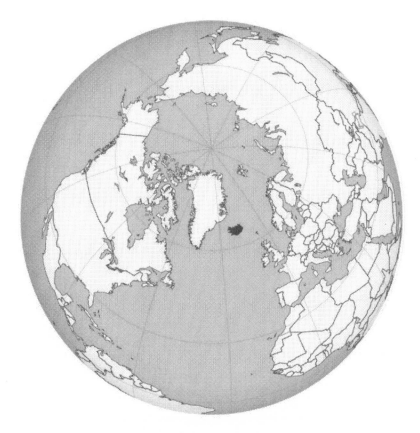

Iceland on the Globe (Greenland Centred)

I HAD read about Iceland during the global financial crisis of 2008, and of how that country had prosecuted the perpetrators of the banking crisis. The people who had lent money to those who didn't have the means to pay it back. The perpetrators all ended up in jail. And so, I was inspired to visit and find out more about this land of integrity!

There are only 366,000 Icelanders. They are an amazing, independent people who still speak their own language and have the largest proportion of writers in the world. With strong community ties, they took on the corrupt financiers who operated with impunity in other countries – and won.

Iceland is the only Arctic country without an indigenous people. It was colonised more than a thousand years ago a mixed population of Celtic and Scandinavian settlers, of which only the Scandinavian cultural element has survived.

Coming from New Zealand, I was struck by some parallels. Iceland is about the same size as the mountainous South Island of New Zealand, itself an isolated oceanic country. Another thing that Iceland also has in common is a young, woman Prime Minister elected in the same year as New Zealand's Jacinda Ardern, namely, Katrín Jakobsdóttir.

But Iceland is much closer to the polar circle, to the lands of perpetual day in summer and perpetual night in winter, than New Zealand. You can cross the Arctic Circle on the island of Grimsey, a bit more than forty kilometres or twenty-five miles north of the main island of Iceland. And yes, Iceland really is named after ice: The country's official Icelandic name, Ísland, does not mean 'island' in Icelandic but land of *ís*, that is to say, ice. Much of Iceland's land surface is covered in glaciers and volcanic desert, with mossy meadows around the coast. There is very little forest.

It was a source of complete admiration and intrigue for me that the Icelanders had made a go of such a place. To survive in such a harsh and remote land is a feat today. But in the early days, without the technologies we have now, it would have been even more so.

In this book, I will describe a road trip around Iceland, a great road trip far more adventurous than most Icelandic tourism, which sticks closely to the region around the capital city of Reykjavík.

And I will also include some information about the Vikings and the traditional Viking folk tales, which almost died out on the mainland of Europe, but which were preserved in Iceland as the Icelandic sagas.

Along with the old Viking religion, the Icelandic sagas are the inspiration behind J. R. R. Tolkien's *Lord of the Rings* and C. S. Lewis's Narnia books. That gives you some idea of what they are like!

And so, I now turn to the first chapter of this book, which introduces you to Iceland and to my first impressions, in much more detail!

CHAPTER 1

Iceland: The only country where whale hunting and whale watching go side by side

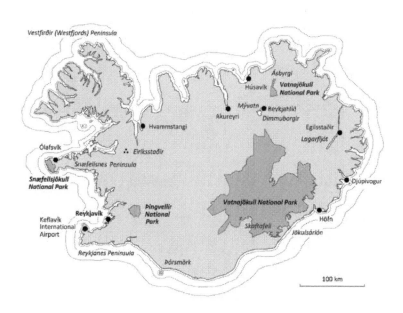

Iceland

ICELAND! So many people asked me 'Why Iceland?' when I told them I was headed there. Well, it was simple. I wanted to go to a country that had told the International Monetary Fund where to go!

How to get there? Easy. I bought a return plane ticket from Auckland, New Zealand to Barcelona, flying British Airways, and then from Barcelona to Reykjavík, flying Vueling. You could also fly to Amsterdam return from Auckland for NZ $1,700 and then, if you had time, take a ferry from Amsterdam to the Faroe Islands and then on to Reykjavík. There are all sorts of other connections and it's not really an epic at all.

Keflavík International Airport, where I arrived, is about fifty kilometres from Reykjavík, the small but popular capital of Iceland. Reykjavík is home to two-thirds of the country's population if we include its outlying villages and towns, and also contains Prime Minister Katrín Jakobsdóttir's constituency.

A Land of Fire, as well as Ice — and some Greenery!

Keflavík is also on the Reykjanes Peninsula, in the news lately because of the eruption of the Fagradalsfjall volcano after nearly eight hundred years of no volcanic eruptions on the peninsula and many thousands of years of Fagradalsfjall's own dormancy.

Eruption at Geldingadalir, one of the peaks of Fagradalsfjall. Photo by 'Berserkur', 24 March 2021, CC BY-SA 4.0 via Wikimedia Commons.

There is just about always a volcano erupting somewhere or other in Iceland, every two years on average. Before Fagradallsfjall, there was the larger eruption at Eyafjallajökull in 2010, which shut down air travel over much of Europe for weeks for fear that the ash plume would damage aircraft engines. Before that, in 1973, a new volcano named Eldfell forced the temporary evacuation of Heimaey, the only permanently inhabited island in the Vestmannaeyjar, Icelandic for 'Irishman Islands'. And that is to list only a few of the most newsworthy eruptions of the last fifty-odd years!

Along with plagues such as the late-mediaeval Black Death and an outbreak of smallpox in the early 1700s, volcanic eruptions have also caused much devastation and loss of life in Iceland. The most fatal volcanic event was a long-continuing eruption of the volcano Laki throughout the second half of 1783 and on into early 1784, forming a string of craters called the Lakagígar (Laki's Craters). The eruption damaged farmland and lead to mass starvation. Indeed, about nine thousand Icelanders starved to death or otherwise perished because of the Lakagígar eruptions, out of a population of around fifty thousand at the time. This event came to be known in Iceland as the 'Mist Hardships' because of the hazy, poisonous vapours the volcano emitted.

Nor was the starvation confined to Iceland. Due to the blotting-out of the sun by volcanic mists, famine and hardship were experienced around the Northern Hemisphere, with severe effects even in distant places.

For instance, perhaps as many as a sixth of the population of Egypt perished due to a failure of the Nile floods that scientists have linked to the Lakagígar eruption's effects on rainfall patterns in Africa. The peasants and townsfolk of France also suffered hardships that may have contributed to the French Revolution of 1789.

Icelandic eruptions can thus have global effects, in ways that remind us of how much things are interconnected and also of how precarious normal life, and for that matter a normal climate, can be.

Moreover, Iceland's volcanoes erupt often. There is a volcanic eruption every two years on average in Iceland. Volcanic eruptions in Iceland are thus not once-in-a-lifetime events, but continual and routine.

And this is because the country is on the mid-Atlantic Ridge: a massive geological feature from which the two sides of the Atlantic Ocean are diverging along with their associated tectonic plates, the various sections into which the Earth's crust is divided. As the crust spreads apart, molten volcanic lava wells up and creates new rock, by way of volcanic eruptions.

In Iceland the two plates that are spreading apart are called the North American Plate, which includes much of North America, and the Eurasian Plate which includes much of Europe and Asia. People therefore like to say that part of Iceland is in America and the other part in Europe from a geological point of view, even if the whole country is considered to be in Europe from a political and cultural point of view.

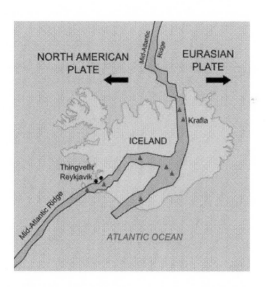

Map showing the Mid-Atlantic Ridge splitting Iceland and separating the North American and Eurasian Plates. The map also shows Reykjavik, the capital of Iceland, the Thingvellir area, and the locations of some of Iceland's active volcanoes (red triangles), including Krafla. Public domain image (1999) from the US Geological Service, via Wikimedia Commons, whence also the map description.

Iceland's more or less continual form of volcanism is similar to what goes on elsewhere along the ridge, but underwater, where because of the pressure of the water it takes a less explosive form. The molten lava simply extrudes into the cold seawater and solidifies at once.

A high level of volcanic activity also means that Iceland has many hot springs, some of which are good for bathing, while others are tapped for geothermal power and home heating.

In some of the places where the mid-Atlantic Ridge crosses Iceland, there are narrow fissures of which people like to say that America is on one side and Europe on the other. One of these is the Silfra Fissure just outside Reykjavík, which is filled with absolutely clear freshwater. Diving tours are organised both with scuba gear for experienced divers, and with snorkels for ordinary folk.

Bridging the nominal divide between America and Europe at the Silfra Fissure. Photo by Ex nihil, 11 June 2014, CC BY-SA 4.0 via Wikimedia Commons.

The Silfra Fissure, which first appeared after an earthquake in 1789, widens by around two to two-and-a-half centimetres a year; so, it will not be possible to bridge it with both arms, as a diver is doing in the photo above, for much longer in that spot! On the Reykjanes Peninsula, southwest of Reykjavík, a continuation of the same crack is spanned by the Leif the Lucky Bridge, also known as the bridge between continents.

'Leif the Lucky Bridge: Bridge between continents in Reykjanes peninsula, southwest Iceland across the Alfagja rift valley, the boundary of the Eurasian and North American continental tectonic plates.' Photo by Chris 73, 25 June 2006, CC BY-SA 3.0 via Wikimedia Commons. Surplus white sky has been trimmed out for this post and emphasis removed from the first four words of the title.

Because of all the volcanic activity associated with seafloor spreading, as well as the Arctic cold which has led to part of the interior being covered by the icecaps that help to give the country its name, only a fifth of Iceland is habitable.

Having said that, the parts that are habitable, generally near the coast, are quite green. That is because Iceland is warmed by the Irminger

Current, a branch of the Gulf Stream. There is no shortage of trees in Reykjavik, for example, as well as in some sheltered valleys and coastal towns elsewhere.

'View from the top of Ásbyrgi canyon. Hiking trail from Dettifoss to Ásbyrgi, Iceland'. Photo by Michal Klajban, 27 July 2017, CC BY-SA 4.0 via Wikimedia Commons.

I even thought that Iceland and neighbouring Greenland — where you are much less likely to come across a tree than in Iceland — should change names!

A Viking-Celtic Colony

Along with volcanoes and hot springs, Iceland also has a rich, long history. Much of that history is recorded in the famous Icelandic sagas, a series of books of mythology and stories from Iceland's early Viking era. In fact, the Icelandic sagas preserve much of what we know about the culture of the Viking era in general.

After the Danes, Swedes and Norwegians became Christians they became inclined to forget about that old stuff ('we're civilised Europeans now') and lost touch with their older, pagan culture. It survived, however, in the Icelandic sagas.

Because of Iceland's remote location and harsh climate, it was one of the last places in the world to become inhabited by people. Norse settlement is thought to have begun around 870 CE, and this is also thought to be the first peopling of the island, or at any rate the first peopling of which there is reliable evidence.

There may also have been a handful of Irish religious hermits in Iceland before that date. If so, they would have chosen a first-rate place to get away from the temptations of what passed for civilisation in Western Europe at the time. A first-rate place to get away from it all, at least until the Vikings showed up to spoil the party. Or rather to get the party going, more like.

In the Viking Age, the Scandinavians, also known then as the Norse, all spoke one language — Old Norse — which diverged from more southerly Germanic dialects, such as the Anglo-Saxon ones that would go on to become the main ancestor of English, sometime around 500 CE.

The word Viking is thought to come from the Old Norse and modern Icelandic word for a coastal bay or inlet, *vík,* either from a general association of bays and inlets with seafaring or from the fact that the

Skagerrak, the huge bay that forms the approaches to Norway, Denmark and Sweden from the North Sea, used to be known to locals simply as 'the Bay'.

Certainly, in its day, the word *viking* referred to the activity of those who set sail in search of adventure, trade, and plunder. In Old Norse, *viking* was a verb form. As we go hiking or biking, the Norse used to go viking!

To speak of a Viking as a person, in the day, the Norse used the masculine noun *vikingr*, meaning 'vikinger' or he who went viking; its plural was *vikingar* or men who went viking. If you wanted to talk about a viking's possessions, you used *vikings*. Like many European languages, apart from English, Old Norse routinely assigned gender to nouns, no doubt realistically so in the case of the *vikingar*.

Runestone at Rök, Sweden

Photo by Bengt Olof Åradsson (2004), CC BY 1.0 via Wikimedia Commons

After Iceland was colonised, Old Norse diverged into a variety of languages that today include Danish, Swedish, Norwegian, Icelandic and Faroese, the language of the Faroe Islands, which lie between Scotland and Iceland.

Of all these closely related languages, Icelandic is the one that is still closest to Old Norse.

Old Norse was originally written in runes, the strange, scratch-like alphabet that you find on many standing stones in northern Europe, like the one on the preceding page.

Modern Icelandic, and historical Old Norse texts today, are written in a Latin alphabet similar to that of English, but with some accents and dots on top of the vowels that modify their pronunciation, a run-together æ as in Danish, and also the highly distinctive characters ð, which never appears at the start of a word but which is written Ð if the whole word is in capital letters, and another symbol written þ in lower case and Þ as a capital. These are called eth and thorn respectively.

Eth and thorn represent 'th' sounds that also exist in English, but which have died out in Norwegian, Danish and Swedish. Eth is th as in 'that', while thorn is usually pronounced as in 'through' or 'thick'. In Iceland, the letter name eth is written as eð and thorn is written as þorn.

It is easy for a modern English-speaker to mistake thorn for a 'p', and eth for a 'd', so these are both something to watch out for.

In fact, thorn and eth used to exist in English as well. Eth died out in English with the coming of print, as there was no such letter in typesets imported from Continental Europe. Thorn survived for another couple of

16

hundred years but was represented by the letter Y/y, the letter I/i being used where we would now write Y/y.

That is where the myth that people said 'ye' for 'the' in older forms of English comes from. A myth that one scholarly blogger rather wittily calls 'Ye Old Mispronunciation': I hat-tip that post in the references at the end of this chapter. Anyway, the Icelanders, though few, were more stubborn than the British and insisted on the manufacture of typesets that did contain eth and thorn.

It seems that when the Norse arrived in Iceland, they also brought slaves from raids in Ireland and Scotland with them. Certainly, they brought women from Ireland and Scotland. 62% of Icelanders' maternal genetics are of Gaelic and Celtic descent, which is much higher than other Scandinavian countries, while the paternal genetic pool is dominated by Norse genes.

In old Norse, the Celtic peoples, above all those Celts with whom the Norse had most interaction, namely the Irish and the closely related Scots Gaels (themselves from Ireland) were called Vestmenn, or 'west men'. This was because Ireland and all the other areas where Celts were found were to the west of European Scandinavia. The Icelanders retain the same term, though of course Iceland is further west still. Whence, the Vestmannaeyjar.

It was all stuff I found completely fascinating! As I also found some of the similarities between Icelandic and English, similarities which can partly be explained by the fact that Old Norse was related to Anglo-Saxon. And by the fact that after Great Britain was colonised by the Anglo-Saxons, parts of modern-day Ireland, Scotland and northern England were then colonised by the Vikings as well.

Why I went

As I mentioned at the start, one of the main reasons I went to Iceland was because of their response to the 2008 financial crisis. The Icelandic economy was doing quite well until then. When the financial crisis happened, the Icelandic government refused to bail out the banks and in doing so showed favour to the taxpayers over the banks.

This, of course, caused an international stir. Iceland even went as far as prosecuting and jailing four businessmen who were responsible for lending more money than they ever should have. Unlike other countries suffering from the recession Iceland made hardly any cuts to social welfare payments. I had to admire them for that.

I also wanted to find out how they survived — how did people in Iceland make their money?

Cool Reykjavík

The capital city, Reykjavík, was the first part of the country that I explored. It was one of the cleanest, safest and most prosperous-looking cities I had ever visited. There were few signs that the nation had been in financial difficulties.

Reykjavík overlooked to Esja or Esjan (the Esja), the mountain range just north-east of the city.

Reykjavík is a hugely popular tourist destination, and tourism counts as the second largest source of income for Iceland. So, maybe that helped.

I went in the off season as I knew how busy it got, and I wanted an experience without the overloading of tourists. It was a deliberate endeavour to give myself more of a chance to meet the locals and see what happened outside of the busy season.

As I was driving around the city, I noticed how many of the buildings were made from driftwood and corrugated iron. Apparently, that was how everything had looked prior to the modernisation of the city.

19

Reykjavík

*Hallgrimskirkja
(Church of
Hallgrímur)*

I arrived on a Sunday. I didn't have much to do that day, so I took myself to an 11 a.m. sermon at Hallgrimskirkja: what better way to meet the locals. It was a Lutheran church, and a very simple one at that. No stained-glass windows or gilding inside. The church was quite fascinating.

It was a modern building, with a tower over seventy metres high. It was the largest church in all Iceland. It took over forty years to build and was finally completed in 1986. It was then named after the seventeenth-century Lutheran preacher Hallgrimur Petursson, the author of a body of work called the Passion Hymns.

The pipe organ, purchased from generous donations from the community, was probably the only decorative thing within the church. I enjoyed it though and mingled with a few of the locals after the service. The language wasn't a barrier either, as most people were bilingual and spoke both Icelandic and English.

My accommodation was simple and modest: a hostel in Reykjavík that only cost US $50 a night. It had a double bed. Thankfully it was really warm, and so comfortable! I noticed that the advertisement for the hostel showed an Icelandic mother and her child who were meant to live in the hostel.

I found out though that it was managed by an American, who really didn't want to be bothered. I was trying to get some printouts of mortgage documents, thanks to my ongoing Queenstown drama, and they didn't want to help me there, so I crossed the road to the Bus Hostel — they were fabulous! Even though I wasn't staying there they helped me print off everything I needed. Next time I go to Iceland I will be staying there! Good customer service goes a long way.

I went to the local tourist office to get a map of the whole country, so I could plan what I was going to do. Surprisingly enough I wasn't able to get one, so I downloaded one off Lonely Planet instead. I needed to see what I was going to do and the approximate times it would take to travel by car.

I was going to hire a car as there were no trains or other forms of long-distance public transport to get around, as far as I could tell. I didn't want to do a coach tour either. I get bored very easily, so I wanted to plan everything that *I* wanted to do, not tag along with a bunch of gaggling tourists. I wanted extreme adventure — I thrived on it.

One thing I loved about Reykjavík was the outdoor art sculptures around the town. There were even a few sculpture trails that ran through the central city, and I stumbled upon heaps of great outdoor art works. I loved the simple themes of love and landscape that was evident in them all. I also found the Einar Jonsson art museum, home to a range of classical sculptures surrounded by park-like settings.

Einar Jonsson was Iceland's very first sculptor, and he lived in the house, that then became the museum, until his death in 1954.

I found the Sun Voyager Sculpture, Sólfar, down by the Reykjavík waterfront not too far from Opera House. It is a stunning outdoor sculpture of a boat, crafted by the artist Jón Gunnar Árnason, said to be a monument to the sun. He also described it is a boat of hope, the future, and exploration of undiscovered territories.

Reykjavík was filled with museums, so I was in my element. I did the Iceland Art Museum, the Modern Art Museum — that was very cool — and an old Viking Long House in Hofsstaðir Historic Park. The National Museum of Iceland in Reykjavík showed me the history of Iceland through art, sculptures, and exhibitions.

*There are lots more
sculptures in Reykjavik!*

Paintings in the Reykjavík Art Museum

Sólfar sculpture, Reykjavík.
Pixabay public domain image by MsKayWu

*Perlan ('The Pearl'), an important museum of the
Wonders of Iceland, revolving restaurant and lookout
overlooking Reyjkjavík.*

English Wikipedia image (April 2013) by Tanya Hart, CC-BY-SA 2.0.

26

The National Museum was where I learned that the first settlers to Iceland were from Norway, with a large admixture of Celts from the British Isles.

The harbour in Reykjavík was a great spot to hang out and I spent a lot of time there, strolling along the waterfront and captivated by the icebergs out at sea. There were plenty of whale-watching boats for tourists anchored there, alongside whale-hunting boats.

Food Traditions

I was found the takeaway bar where Bill Clinton ate a hot dog in 2004! Apparently, it was such a big deal they named a mustard-only one after him. I didn't feel appetized enough to eat a Bill Clinton hot dog, so I carried on walking. Actually, I should have had one, but with the five traditional condiments: mustard, tomato sauce, crispy fried onions, fresh onions, and remoulade, a yellow, gherkiny sauce that's a mixture of mustard and what we call picallili. Icelandic hot dogs (pulser or pylser, from the word for sausage) are supposed to be about the best in the world, with real German-cum-Scandinavian-cum-Icelandic style sausages; and only picky foreigners refuse the traditional ladling of all five condiments.

And hot dogs, as it turns out, are the traditional local fast food, what fish and chips are to the North Sea coastal towns of England and Scotland and used to be in New Zealand as well, before we were invaded by American fast-food chains. Well, at least when it comes to hot dog stands, the Icelanders thought of it first and continue to hold their own.

Traditional Icelandic foods that are perhaps a bit more of an acquired taste, or otherwise take getting used to, include boiled sheep's heads, known as svið, and 'rotten' shark. Safe to say I wasn't going to eat that last one either, though it's not really rotten but rather, fermented. It sounded a lot like the Greenlanders' kiviak routine. The Icelanders call it kæstur hákarl and it consists of shark meat that is left to cure in a hole buried under gravel, and then hung to dry for 4–5 months. Sorry I'm not that game. But then everyone I talked to who was from Iceland didn't really eat it either!

Apparently, like the tremendously off-putting kiviak, which looks like month-old roadkill and can be fatal if improperly prepared, kæstur hákarl is something of an acquired taste. Anthony Bourdain called kæstur hákarl "the single worst, most disgusting and terrible tasting thing" he had ever eaten; but then again, I don't know whether he ever had kiviak, which *looks* more disgusting (if not quite as disgusting as Sardinian maggot cheese). On the other hand, they say the first time with kæstur hákarl is the worst but then you get to like it. Or so they say. And so I am told. Furthermore, kæstur hákarl has the advantage over kiviak that not only is it safer to eat (probably), but also, it doesn't look like decaying roadkill.

Like many of the cultures living near the Arctic Circle, the people of Iceland have depended a lot upon the sea as a source of food that was more reliable, under the conditions in which they lived, than farming. The vile nature and dodgy methods of preservation of many of their 'acquired taste' foods also speaks volumes about past hardship and unwillingness to throw things out, and not just in the Arctic either. Imagine how desperate the first French person to consume blue vein or a 'runny' soft cheese must have been; not to mention the first Sardinian to sample their even more extreme delicacy.

Besides the rotten shark and the boiled sheep's heads there were other foods of a more normal nature in today's Iceland. I've mentioned the hot dogs. Smoked lamb was the base of a beautiful, rich and flavoursome meal that I had somewhere in my Icelandic travels. Salt fish was also a popular food, I found. I remember they had it in Greenland too — it's really just a small heavily salted fish that tastes just that — salty fish. In Icelandic they call it saltfiskur and in Greenlandic they call it ammassat.

The Icelanders also used to eat whales, and still consume seals. So, I decided to find out what the policies were today with regard to marine mammals.

First off, no polar bears are allowed into the country. If and when they arrive on drifting ice and start roaming around looking for something to eat, they are shot. Iceland has no qualms about shooting them on sight, something I really disagree with. I'm not saying all Icelanders agree either: but that's just the policy. They are considered dangerous to humans and livestock and are immediately dealt with just like that. Actually, there have only been a few sightings of polar bears in modern-day Iceland, although the melting of the polar ice may be making this rare event less rare. The last sighting of a polar bear in Iceland was in 2016 (shot dead) and, before that, in 2010.

Between the rarity of their arrival and the usual response, you will hardly ever see a living polar bear in Iceland: and the local policy is to keep it that way, so that everyone can sleep soundly. In places like Greenland, of course, people have had to get used to having them around. And in the northern Canadian town of Churchill, they do polar bear tours!

If a negative policy toward the polar bear is an occasional issue, Icelandic whaling has had more widespread media attention across the world. I mentioned a worldwide ban on whaling earlier; but there are a handful of non-compliant exceptions and once again, as with the polar bears, Iceland is one of them, the other being Japan with its 'scientific' whaling. It seems to be more trouble than it is worth for Iceland, particularly so given that the Icelandic whaling industry is just a shadow of what it once was (thankfully).

Icelandic whaling boats have been sabotaged by Greenpeace activists and their Rainbow Warrior. In 1989 Greenpeace even organised boycotts of all Icelandic fishing exports, which led to fast food outlets like Wendy's and Long John Silver cancelling their contracts with Icelandic suppliers.

As of the time of writing, in late 2021, the Icelandic whaling fleet is tied up and inactive, but it is possible that it might still resume its activities.

As with fermented shark, the Icelanders don't really eat whale any more these days. Apparently, it's the same in Japan. So, a lot of the whales that are caught end up in pet food. Both in Iceland and Japan, it seems that some kind of weird murky politics lies behind the persistence of an industry that just about everyone apart from the whalers themselves now seems to regard as a complete anachronism.

Sealing is another old-timey industry that seems to be on the way out, increasingly in tension with seal-watching. I popped into an actual seal museum in Hvammstangi, on my drive around the coast. It was interesting, and it highlighted the historic dependence of Icelanders on the animal.

From Foundation to Independence, and Beyond

In 874 a Norseman called Ingólfur Arnarsson founded Reykjavík, which is also believed to be the first permanent settlement in Iceland. Erik the Red, who founded Greenland, was also an Icelander.

Around the year 1000, Christianity was adopted by Iceland's population, which had grown to 30,000 or so by then. Christianity was brought to Iceland by Irish monks. The Icelandic sagas refer to the 'Papar' monks or Christians who wandered around the land preaching and lived in some of the villages. These Papar are also mentioned in the histories of the Faroe Islands.

Iceland was ruled by Norway from 1262 to 1380 and then by the Danes from 1380 until the twentieth century, when it gained its modern independence.

Iceland gained Home Rule autonomy in 1904, and then became effectively independent of Denmark in 1918 in the form of a constitutional monarchy in personal union with Denmark, meaning that it shared the same monarch in the manner that New Zealand does with the United Kingdom.

After European Denmark was invaded by the Nazis on the 9th of April 1940, Iceland was bloodlessly occupied by British Commonwealth forces a day later, to prevent the Nazi occupation from extending to this strategic outpost in the North Atlantic.

In July 1941, the defence of Iceland passed to the Americans, who were neutral at the time, an occupation which reverted to a combatant status once the Americans entered World War II in December 1941. Iceland formally declared itself a republic in 1944 after a constitutional referendum which yielded an incredibly popular result, the republic and its proposed constitution each obtaining more than 98% support on a similarly high turnout. The referendum and its result were unpopular with many Danes, who saw the whole thing as a bit of a stab in the back given that they themselves were still under Nazi occupation.

All the same, though some Danes thought it disloyal, the referendum wasn't really a bolt from the blue, as the terms of Iceland's independence in 1918, the Danish-Icelandic Act of Union, had placed Iceland's constitutional status up for review in the early 1940s in any case. The King of Denmark, who had now ceased to be the King of Iceland, sent his congratulations.

I went to see the House of Höfði, which was the British Embassy in the 1950s. The House of Höfði, or Höfði House, is more famous for being the place where the discussions took place between Presidents Reagan and Gorbachev that eventually led to the end the Cold War. Like many of the buildings in Iceland it was quite simple from the outside. There were no formal gardens or manorial extravagance. It was a simple white two storey … well, house, really.

Iceland joined NATO, the North Atlantic Treaty Organisation, as a founding member in 1949.

As a NATO member, Iceland used to host an American military air base at Keflavík, next to the civilian airport of the same name, which is Iceland's largest and the one that most international passengers fly in and out of.

The airport at Keflavík, a name that means driftwood bay, was first built by the Americans as a military airfield during World War II. Part of it was then divided off for the civilian airport. The Americans handed the remaining military base over to the Icelanders in 2006.

The famous Höfði House, where Ronald Reagan and Mikhael Gorbachev negotiated in 1986

33

Iceland's comparatively youthful Prime Minister Katrín Jakobsdóttir, who was elected to that office in 2017, the same year as New Zealand's Jacinda Ardern, leads a party called the Left-Green Movement. Part of their policy is that Iceland should pull out of NATO, and the party also opposes the idea of Iceland becoming a full member of the European Union (it is not a full member at present, but strongly associated all the same.)

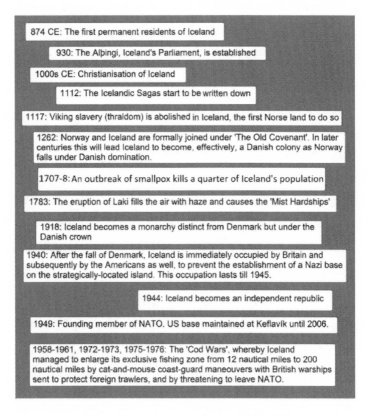

Some key dates in the history of Iceland

Perhaps because of its own independence-struggles as a small nation, Iceland became the first country in the world to officially recognise Lithuania, Estonia and Latvia's independence after the fall of the Soviet Union.

What's the latest about Iceland? Well, in 2017 the same year that Katrín Jakobsdóttir became Prime Minister, Iceland's supreme court ruled that women cannot routinely be prevented from going bare breasted in public swimming pools. The judges said that such bans potentially amount to a form of discrimination and that local councils would therefore have to *prove* that women going topless were indecent if they wished to impose a ban; they couldn't just say they were indecent!

My historical timeline, above, mentions the 'cod wars' with Britain, a long-running fisheries dispute — though not the swimming pool dispute!

A Literate Culture

I also found it amazing that Iceland has the largest percentage of officially recognised writers, per capita, in the world! One in ten Icelanders will write a published book, and many of their past and present authors are world-famous, right up to the level of the Nobel Prize for Literature awarded to novelist Halldór Laxness in 1955.

Just lately, the autobiography of Heida Ásgeirsdottír has made headlines. Ms Ásgeirsdottír was brought up on a sheep-farm that had been in her family since the Middle Ages and worked in New York as a model for a while before returning to the farm when her father got sick. Then she learned of a plan to flood the valley in which the farm was located and turn it into a hydroelectric reservoir. She successfully fought the hydro scheme and became a politician for the Icelandic Green Party for a while. I enjoyed reading her book, *Heida: A Shepherd at the Edge of the World.*

By the way, if you wonder why all the women seem to be called somebody or other's 'dóttir', well, that is because they are. With a few exceptions, the modern Icelanders retain the old European custom of not having family surnames but simply being named after one's father, along with one's own name of course.

Most commonly, the boys just get called whoever-their-father-was's-son, while the girls are similarly named as their father's 'dóttir'. So, the full name of the most famous Icelandic singer is Björk Guðmundsdóttir.

The last Anglo-Saxon king, the one that got the arrow in the eye at the Battle of Hastings, was similarly called Harold Godwinson after his father, Godwin. The sorts of unchanging family surnames that we are used to didn't come into regular use in Britain for another couple of hundred years after King Harold's demise. And in Iceland they never came into general use.I thought it remarkable that the Icelanders were able to hold onto their Norse language through more than five centuries of Danish rule. There was probably less difference between Icelandic and Norwegian during the period of Norwegian rule in the Middle Ages. But the Icelandic language could easily have died out under the Danes as the world grew more modern and as book-learning spread.

After the Normans conquered England, the original Anglo-Saxon tongue of the English gave way to modern English: a language that combines Anglo-Saxon words for common, everyday things with Norman French in areas related to book-learning.

In a similar vein, the Icelanders might well have kept all the words in their language that were identical to Danish ones and replaced the ones that weren't with Danish terms learnt from books, and thus ended up speaking Danish.

So, it was by no means inevitable that ordinary Icelanders of the 21st century would still to be able to read sagas written in the language of the founders of their country. In England, the old Anglo-Saxon language is a dead one read only by people with an academic interest.

It seemed to me that this explained the Icelandic passion for books and for local publishing. The people had been kept from becoming Danish by a local literature written and published in Icelandic. The pen was not only mightier than the sword in the Icelandic independence-struggle but in fact the chief weapon.

Although Danish rule in Iceland wasn't as oppressive as Norman rule in Britain, the Danes did do some things that caused objection locally.

Thus, for instance, in 1602, Denmark ruled that Iceland was not allowed to trade with other countries except Denmark; so, no new ships were built in Iceland. This was a huge loss and demoralisation for the country, lasting until the eighteenth century when Denmark allowed Iceland to trade with other countries again.

In the nineteenth and twentieth centuries, protests and independence movements began to take hold, until the republic finally came in 1944.

I learnt more about all this history after I got a bit bored and decided to head out on a guided tour around the city to see anything I might have missed. Tour guides and touring do have their uses — they are locals and have a lot of knowledge to share. The tour guide, Aaron had boasted of an education system that achieves 100% literacy. It was Aaron who also told me that ten per cent of Icelandic people end up publishing at least one book. The land of poets and sagas!

Apparently, there are quite a few well-known and popular writers' retreats all over Iceland, and people come to them from around the world.

There were three main types of writing during the Mediaeval period, which was an influential time for writers in Iceland. These were the Eddas, Skaldic Poetry and of course the sagas. The literature of Mediaeval Iceland is distinguished by a mixture of romanticism and realistic descriptions of landscapes, nature and people. It was all really interesting, and I got to see some old manuscripts first-hand at a museum that held the historic Icelandic literature. As we were continued on this tour, I noticed that there were a lot of bookstores, cafés and libraries around Reykjavík city centre. Aaron, our tour guide also told us that, apparently, in the very far north of the country there was a school that only had one student and one teacher.

Perhaps the most famous Icelandic expression is 'þetta reddast', meaning 'this will be alright'. It's supposed to reflect the idea that the Icelanders are a nation of hardy stoics with honest values, who can mend anything and are unfazed by anything and who all pitch in to help — volcanic eruptions, roads blocked by snow, come what may. Whatever happens, they'll fix it somehow. New Zealanders used to have an expression that was just the same, namely, 'she'll be right'. Whatever happened, the resourceful Kiwis would improvise a solution, too.

But then the New Zealand version started to acquire connotations of slackness and the covering-up of risk and fell out of use. People started to think that things wouldn't be alright. The answer to 'She'll be right?', stated as a question, became 'Yeah, right!' I don't know if any similar disillusionment now dogs the meaning of þetta reddast; or whether people really do believe in it still.

Something else I found really interesting is that, while most of the population in Iceland claim to be Lutheran, there is a revival of the Norse folk religion called the Asatru Fellowship or in Icelandic, Ásatrúarfélagið. It is based around the connection Icelanders have with the land and spiritual forces and includes stories about elves and dwarves, stories that I would hear more about on my journey as I went past places that are spoken about in the old myths and legends.

Would I go again?

Yes! Iceland was fabulous — I really loved it! I enjoyed it thoroughly: it was alive and vibrant!

References

Erin Servais, 'Ye Old Mispronunciation: The Long Forgotten Letter "Thorn",' 26 July 2011, on grammarpartyblog.com.

The Anthony Bourdain quote comes from Rachel Herz, 'You eat that?, *Wall Street Journal,* January 28, 2012, accessed 20 October 2021 on URL: web.archive.org/web/20150317012217/https://www.wsj.com/articles/SB10001 4240529702046616045771868843056231170.

For more, see:

a-maverick.com/blog/iceland-whale-hunting-watching

CHAPTER 2

Travel Tips for Iceland

IF you catch a plane to Iceland, the airport at which you will most likely arrive is Keflavík International Airport, on the Reykjanes Peninsula near the capital city of Reykjavík. This is the airport that I arrived at in Chapter One. Three other airports, Reykjavík, Akureyri and Egilsstaðir also take international flights. But unless you are coming in from Greenland or the Faroe Islands, it is a near certainly that your plane will be scheduled to land at Keflavík.

Tourists generally explore Iceland by way of three circular routes. One of them extends right around the main island, and that was the route I took.

The second, but most popular, is a 300-kilometre (186 mile) route starting and ending in Reykjavík, called the Golden Circle, which takes in the city plus three more of the most popular tourist destinations in Iceland. These are, in alphabetical order:

- The Geysir Geothermal Area (whence geyser in English)
- Gullfoss Waterfall, huge and wild; and,
- Þingvellir National Park (also spelt Thingvellir for tourists)

Þingvellir gets its name from the fact that Iceland's parliament, the Althingi, which in Icelandic is written Alþingi first met at the place that would thereafter be known as Þingvellir, in the year 930.

But Þingvellir does not draw the tourists for that these days, so much as for the fact that it is where the great mid-ocean rift that divides Iceland is most visible, including the crystal-clear dive site known as the Silfra Fissure, which continues the rift underwater and which is quite cheap to dive near the surface by snorkel, though scuba divers can go deeper.

I showed a photo of divers in the Silfra Fissure in Chapter One. Here is a photo of Gullfoss!

Gullfoss (foss means waterfall in Icelandic). Photo by Andreas Tille, 30 July 1998, CC BY-SA 4.0 via Wikimedia Commons.

The third circular route is the 250-kilometre or 155-mile Diamond Circle, which takes in some of the attractions of the north-east, and which you might do without venturing further afield if you landed and departed in the north-east, which is trying to develop as a tourism region independent of the Reykjavík area and its Golden Circle. Sights on the Diamond Circle include, in alphabetical order once more,

- Ásbyrgi, a strange horseshoe-shaped canyon with lush vegetation, of which I also showed a photo in Chapter One, on its sheltered floor (byrgi means shelter in Icelandic)

- Dettifoss, said to be the first or second most powerful waterfall in Europe

- Goðafoss, another big waterfall, into which statues of Norse gods were thrown when Iceland became Christian in 1000 CE

- Húsavík, an attractive town on the north coast which is also Iceland's whale-watching capital; and,

- Lake Mývatn, with its beautiful shades of green and blue on a fine day, and the surrounding volcanic area

I ended up doing several of these in the course of my ring-route exploration, in any case.

The places I have just listed are only some of the best-known of Iceland's many incredible attractions. And, in this book, I certainly don't mention everything you could possibly see. Instead, I have listed some sources of information further on in this chapter so that you can do your own research, which I firmly recommend. Not to mention, consulting detailed tourism handbooks of the *Lonely Planet, Fodor's* and *Rough Guide* variety. You really don't want to unwittingly go past something in Iceland, especially on a road trip!

One of the latest attractions, whereby you can take in many of the sights at once, is **FlyOver Iceland: flyovericeland.com.** This is a virtual flight over many of the most scenic parts of Iceland, displayed on a wraparound screen and with tilting seats and wind and scents that make it feel like you are in a plane, made more exciting by the fact that a lot of the footage is filmed from drones shooting through perilous places no aircraft with people inside could actually go. FlyOver Iceland is based on the Reykjavík waterfront.

One of the advantages of taking in a virtual trip like that of FlyOver Iceland is that the weather in Iceland is very changeable and wet, so that when you get to some famous scenic destination, it might be misted out or snowing.

Before the name Iceland was settled upon, the country was also known as Snaeland, meaning land of snow!

Iceland in Winter: NASA public domain image via NASA Earth Observatory

(Iceland has many alternative names, of which Snaeland is just one. Another favourite of mine is Garðarshólmi, Garðar's Island, after the person the sagas name as the leader of the second Viking-era expedition to Iceland.)

Along with lots of ice and snow even in comparatively calm weather, the country is susceptible to terrible storms as well, similar to hurricanes even though it is a long way from the warm waters in which hurricanes usually form. In another interesting NASA photograph, you can see the edge of neighbouring Greenland marked out as a dark line through the edge of one such storm, which looks like something out of *The Day After Tomorrow.*

'Low off Iceland': NASA public domain image (photographed 4 September 2003), via NASA Visible Earth.

The strait between Iceland and Greenland is one of the stormiest and windiest places in the world, and the bad weather often spills over onto the land. Which is bad enough: but imagine being in a Viking longship halfway between Iceland and Greenland when something like that brewed up—I think the voyage would have ended in Valhalla!

Not surprisingly, then, the roads in Iceland can be treacherous, what with high winds, bad weather, ice, snow, and on top of that, wild animals and livestock wandering about, the chief hazard being that you may run into them.

Another peculiar hazard is that of the volcanic dust storm, also known as a sandstorm or ash storm. This can happen in many places but is most likely to be serious on the south coast. In Chapter Five, I talk about an encounter with one such storm.

It pays to get Sand and Ash Protection (SAAP) insurance for any vehicle you rent because, apart from the risk of being blown off the road or having a door wrenched off or window blown in, such a storm may also sandblast the paintwork and glazing on your rental. This kind of insurance may be covered in your rental agreement, but it is best to check in any case. And also to follow the weather forecasts carefully for wind warnings.

The ring route around the main island, and the roads near Reykjavík, are quite good, but the roads into the interior are generally rougher, only to a four-wheel drive standard in places, and often closed in winter as well. Unless you are a local acquainted with the back country, it generally does not pay to try and take a shortcut through the middle of Iceland.

A further reason to avoid random journeys into the interior is that mobile phone coverage is patchy to non-existent once you get into remote areas.

The gnarly conditions that exist across much of the country probably explain why so many tourists stick close to Reykjavik and the Golden Circle. All the same, if you do the big road trip around the country like I did, you come across lots of interesting things that you would never see on the usual tourist trail! And you won't be bothered by too many other tourists either.

To continue, in Iceland, it pays to submit your travel itinerary with someone who will make sure that you will be searched for if you don't turn up. The SafeTravel App and website are one such place where plans can be submitted. Details of these are furnished below.

The emergency phone number in Iceland is **112,** and there is also an app based on this number where you can just push a virtual button.

It also pays to get a local SIM card for your mobile phone, although some European plans also work in Iceland without roaming charges. There are three local mobile phone providers of which, according to the website of the tour operator Intrepid Travel, for which I provide details below, Siminn apparently provides the widest coverage in remote areas as of the time of writing (2021).

You can pick up a local SIM on arrival at Keflavík International Airport, and presumably also at the other airports of international arrival.

In case you don't want to go by road (there are no railways in Iceland), there is also a very rich network of domestic air routes, with just about every corner of the country having a domestic airport, A full list of Icelandic airports and air routes is provided on the website of Iceland's air transport authority Isavia: **Isavia.is**.

The currency used in Iceland is the Icelandic Króna, which appears as 'kr' on shop signs, and is currently worth a little over one New Zealand cent or a little less than one US cent. Posted prices in 'kr' are thus not as expensive as they look! Visa and Mastercard are widely accepted as of the time of writing, as are Euro and US dollar notes in some city businesses, but Icelandic paper money is a good idea for remote areas. *(Source: Icelandontheweb.com)*

Useful apps for Iceland, mostly free or freemium, include:

- 112 Iceland (emergency services app based on the 112 number, which allows you to update your location manually and also to send a distress signal, using the cellphone network. You are advised to use it even if the phone claims to have no signal, as it might still get through.)

- SafeTravel (for travel advisories and for reporting where you intend to go, in case you go missing)

- Veður, the weather app

- Aurora Forecast

- Iceland Road Guide

- Appy Hour (an urban app for Reykjavík)

- Appening Today (another urban app for Reykjavík)

- Vegan Iceland

- WAPP (a very useful hiking app)

- Strætó (public transport)

- Icelandic Phrasebook

- Map of Iceland Offline

- What's On Event Calendar

- Fun Iceland

- CellMapper (useful for determining mobile phone coverage)
- Oanda Currency Converter App

  (Sources, with more information, include: Hostel.is and Whatson.is)

Some useful general websites include:

CellMapper: cellmapper.net. Useful for getting a map of Iceland's mobile phone coverage.

Guide to Iceland: guidetoiceland.is. This website includes an accommodation page, among other tourist information.

Iceland on the Web: icelandontheweb.com. Another useful tourism website.

Hostelling International Iceland: **hostel.is**

SafeTravel: safetravel.is. Advises of travel hazards and is also a website where you can submit your travel plans, so that people will look for you if you don't turn up.

What's On: whatson.is Entertainment guide.

Road information website: road.is Useful for closures and related information.

Bus services: straeto.is/en

Tour operator websites include:

Arctic Adventures: adventures.is. Tour operators and providers of further useful travel information.

Fun Iceland: funiceland.is. Travel, tours and car booking, with an interesting blog as well.

Hey Iceland: heyiceland.is. This site describes travel, tours (including self-driving tours, activities, and accommodation, with an emphasis on out-of-the-way areas.

Icelandic Mountain Guides: **mountainguides.is.** I used this firm when I was in Iceland (see Chapter 5).

Intrepid Travel: intrepidtravel.com/en/Iceland. Tour operators and providers of further useful information.

Lastly, also, the curiously named firm I rented my car from, namely, **SADcars: sadcars.com.**

These lists are surely not exhaustive!

You can also book accommodation in Iceland with Booking.com as well as other general travel and accommodation websites and apps such as Airbnb.

When it comes to **medical matters,** you must have proper travel health insurance.

Apart from that, my loyal travel companion was my medical kit, which along with sticking plasters, bandages and scissors contained the diarrhoea stopper loperamide, some ciprofloxacin antibiotics, packets of Gastrolyte rehydration solution and Tramadol, Tiger Balm, Vaseline for dry skin, tea tree oil, iodine and bandages, and, finally, plain old paracetamol. Not exactly a romantic set-up, but realistic, nonetheless.

And also, be up to date with **vaccinations** before you go, **travel insurance** of every kind, and **travel advisories.**

Lastly, when it comes to Covid restrictions, Iceland was a leader in controlling the outbreaks in 2020, without going so far as to lock down the country and eliminate the virus, as the Icelanders felt that their tourism industry was too important for that. Iceland played a large part in the development of the technique of analysing the different strains so that chains of transmission could be nailed down to point of knowing exactly who gave the disease to whom.

Of late, like a lot of places, Iceland has had an outbreak of the Delta strain, and is struggling to contain that as well, as of the time of writing, though if anyone is going to get on top of things it will probably be the Icelanders.

For more, see:

a-maverick.com/blog/world-travel-tips

CHAPTER 3

The Great Epic Iceland Road Trip: Volcanic dust storms, blizzards, and my first time driving with snow tyres on the right

Route One (Iceland)

Wikimedia Commons image (2004) by Biekko, CC BY-SA 3.0.
This is from the Wikpedia article on Route One. The locations numbered clock-
wise are 1, Reykjavík; 2, Borgarnes; 3, Blönduós; 4, Akureyri; 5, Egilsstaðir; 6.
Höfn; 7. Selfoss.. I went anti-clockwise and visited some of these, plus others.

I HAD not really been keen on the idea of hiring a car to drive myself around Iceland, but it seemed that was going to be my only option. There were no train or bus services that went to the area I most wanted to visit: the Icelandic East Coast. A lot of the roads had cameras on them, I noticed: presumably to keep track of maverick travellers like myself who may go astray with the potential to get lost. I was thankful for that: because it was a new country, and I didn't know the roads. The last thing I wanted to happen was to get stuck out in the ice and snow with no help. Indeed, a lot of the roads do close in winter and are only open in summer, because you just can't get through once the snow arrives.

There are quite a few national parks around Iceland beyond the so-called Golden Triangle or Golden Circle, the short day-tripper sightseeing loop in the Reykjavík region that is all some tourists ever see. The Golden Triangle takes in Þingvellir National Park (a UNESCO World Heritage site), the Great Geysir (or geyser), and the Gullfoss Waterfall, all of them epic attractions and enough for many people of course.

In addition to its historical significance as the site of what is perhaps the world's oldest parliament still in existence today (albeit in abeyance for some of the time since 930 CE), Þingvellir also contains sections of the great mid-Atlantic crack, which because of its straightness almost seems artificial. The result is a line of high, straight, stone walls, with uplifted land on either side and land that has dropped down in between, including the parts that are underwater in the great, crystal-clear Silfra Fissure.

Scientifically speaking, America is on one side of the rift and Europe is on the other. The same, scientific definition puts Greenland in the

Americas, since it's west of the crack. And for that matter the western part of Iceland too, though by convention all Iceland is classed as part of Europe.

Iceland's national parks, Þingvellir included, are popular for outdoor pursuits. You can rock climb, hike and visit the many waterfalls, volcanic landscapes and glaciers. Camping and backpacking seemed to be really popular in Iceland, and I was surprised at how many other people were doing these things even in the off-season!

There used to be four national parks in Iceland, but two, Skaftafell and Jökulsárgljúfur, were merged in 2008 to create Vatnajökull National Park, so now there are three. Still, that's two more than Greenland, even if they're smaller! Iceland also offers nature reserves and protected areas on top of the three national parks. So, there is no shortage of things to do outdoors!

The car I hired was an old white thing that looked like it had seen better days. It was a 1997 Toyota. It wasn't pretty, but I know Toyotas are reliable and trusty, so that made me feel slightly better about the whole thing. I paid US $300 for ten days which I didn't think was too bad from the rental company, SADcars, a name that must have a more cheerful significance in Icelandic. I figured it would take me ten days to drive around the whole country on Route One and enough time to make my stops and treks along the way.

*Landscapes east of Reykjavík
and my trusty car*

Route One is the main road that connects all the main towns around Iceland, it literally does a circle of the whole country – Icelanders also call it the Hringvegur, or Ring Road. Route One is a mostly coastal road, but you still pass by some stunning landscapes like geysers and volcanic mountains. Route One was about 1,340 km long so it really wasn't impossibly far to go by New Zealand standards: roughly the equivalent of driving around the South Island, which is about the same size as Iceland in actual fact.

I had read that weather in Iceland can change in the blink of an eye, and that gusty winds and bad weather can turn a two-hour trip into a five-hour trip quite easily. I checked the daily report on the roads and the forecast weather for the week ahead, and it all looked fine to me. It was unusually cold for this time of year. Summer was coming in, but the warm weather hadn't quite switched on yet.

I wasn't the only one who was a bit confused by the weather, I found. A few rather worried-looking tourists loading their hire cars up with tents and camping equipment, obviously hoping that the weather would not ruin their holidays. I think we must all have been on a summer holiday that's turned into an epic tale of survival – a saga – in the face of rain and floods and the tent being blown down. I know I have.

My itinerary included driving along the East Coast, checking out birds, National Parks and walkways along the way. I was going to drive through all three of the major National Parks, Snæfellsjökull, Þingvellir (which is also spelt Thingvellir) and the huge Vatnajökull.

The word jökull means glacier in Icelandic, the same as the Danish word isbræ, and it's significant that two out of three national parks in Iceland have jökull in their name. Jökull is also cognate with the word 'icicle' in English, in other words the nearest Icelandic equivalent in terms of its linguistic ancestry, and similar sounding as cognates usually are, though the meaning has shifted, and it now means glacier. Anyhow, best to wrap up well when visiting these parks, even in summer!

There were a few nature reserves I wanted to get to as well, in Mývatn and Skaftafell, as well as a glacial lake at Jökulsárlón. Before I left, the woman at SADcars told me to be careful when you get out of the car, that I should hold onto the doors because the winds are very strong and can come out of nowhere and blow the doors out. I looked at the car and figured that had already happened to it more than once!

There was a coding system for the roads too. One or two digits were okay and the old Toyota I had would make it over these fine. Anything with three digits or more was a no-go zone: you would need a four-wheel-drive, the more serious the better, to go on those roads.

Everything was cheap and cheerful at SADcars, no doubt in the view that there was no point sending posh cars over Iceland's rough terrain or they wouldn't stay posh for long. Overall, though, the company was great to deal with. They provided me with a map of the roads, with a key so that you could see which ones were four-wheel drive roads.

At times, it's impossible even for four-wheel-drives to go right through the middle of the island. That's why the Ring Road is so important, even if it is often the long way around.

I felt ready to roll. Let the adventures in Iceland begin!

For more, see:

a-maverick.com/blog/iceland-road-trip-volcanic-dust-storms-blizzards-snow-tyres

CHAPTER 4

The Vikings: Seafarers who hated Fish

THE VIKINGS were probably the most notorious folk to have inhabited the Scandinavian realm. The word conjures up images of warriors sailing forth to wreak havoc on the world. There is a lot that remains from that time: I've seen old Viking longboats in museums across Scandinavia.

As I've mentioned, the Vikings weren't a people as such, so much as old-time Norse or Scandinavians engaged in a mixture of raiding and trading. All the same, historians speak of a Viking Age and a Viking culture, when these practices were more prevalent than either before, when the Scandinavians only paddled about in their home waters, or afterward, when they became Christianised and somewhat less warlike.

The Viking Age is said to have begun with a raid on a monastery on the offshore British island of Lindisfarne in 793 CE. The Viking Age ran, thereafter, through to the 11th century.

Raiding and trading apart, another reason the Vikings set sail over long distances was to find better farming lands. The areas they originally occupied were harsh and the snows and long winters made farming difficult. It is believed that the Vikings were the first Europeans to settle in Canada.

On the positive side, the Vikings really were very good at exploring – they went as far as Canada and Russia and there is evidence that they were in Baghdad. The Vikings sailed right around Europe by way of the internal waterways of Russia, which connected the Baltic Sea to the Black Sea. They were, as such, a common sight on the streets of Constantinople, today's Istanbul. The Eastern Roman (Byzantine) Emperor, who reigned in Constantinople, even employed a bodyguard of Vikings known as the Varangian Guard. Anyone who wanted to harm the emperor had to take on the Vikings first. That must have foiled a few plots!

In their early days the Vikings specialised in plundering wealthy monasteries and churches, so that the Christians thought they were the agents of the Devil. Christianity didn't become widespread among the Norse until the 11th century, though some parts of Scandinavia began converting to Christianity as early as the 8th century.

Because they penetrated so far south and established regular trade routes, the Vikings also brought a measure of Arab and Middle Eastern influence into the heart of Europe. This was mostly a matter of peaceable commerce, with certain northern products such as amber being taken south, and vice versa. One result is that coins bearing Arabic writing continue to be dug up all over Europe to this day, sometimes in large amounts.

The 1999 film *The 13th Warrior,* which stars Antonio Banderas as an Arab scholar attached to a band of Vikings, is loosely based on the reverse penetration of Europe by Middle Eastern traders along Viking routes.

(The Finns were not part of the mainstream of Viking culture. Like the British, they tended to on the receiving end of Viking raids instead.)

As I mentioned in Chapter Two, Viking is really a verb form, denoting the activity of seeking out faraway bays. The old Norse used to say that they were off viking, not that they were Vikings as such. Some also got to go berserk (another Viking word), like this Rook-figure in a chess set discovered on the Scottish Isle of Lewis who is chewing his shield, so keen is he get into the fray.

Berserker Rook, Isle of Lewis Chess Pieces

Berserk comes from the Norse for 'bear shirt'; such elite warriors would sometimes wear a bearskin. The people of the North were chronically afraid of bears, with good reason of course, given the size of the two main species of bear that inhabited the polar regions, the brown or grizzly bear, and the polar bear. Imagine living in some remote collection of huts and having a gigantic bear invade your settlement, intent on eating pretty much whatever it sees. Indeed, so great were these fears that bears and those named after them were often referred to by euphemisms such as bee-wolf (Beowulf, in Anglo-Saxon) and honey-eater (Medved, in Russian) lest speaking the word for bear somehow magically caused one to appear.

So, wearing a bearskin signified fearlessness, not least because some incredibly brave soul had had to get it off the bear in the first place. Remember, guns had not yet been invented. Everything was up close and personal, and even if you shot so large a bear with an arrow from what you thought was a safe distance, most probably all that would do would be to make it come looking for its tormentor.

The Isle of Lewis Berserker, who also seems to sport an early version of Saint Andrew's Cross on his shield, looks comical now. But I don't think that was the intended effect at the time.

To stick with their modern name, the Vikings sailed in distinctive longships with snake- or dragon-headed prows, ships light in weight and with shallow draughts to enable them to penetrate up rivers and estuaries. They bore square sails made of the hairy wool of semi-wild sheep, made windproof with a mixture of fir pitch and grease. The Vikings are also believed to have used ingenious navigation methods ranging from knowledge of currents and the behaviour of birds (who also signified land to the Polynesians) through to proto-scientific instruments and even, most remarkably of all, something called the *sólarsteinn* or sunstone which gave the navigator the power to look through thick cloud to see where the sun was.

This sounds far-fetched, but in fact there are transparent minerals that do have this property. It is to do with the direction of the polarisation of the sun's light. These minerals allow light to pass through selectively, by means of the same principle whereby polarising sunglasses and camera filters screen out the glare that is otherwise reflected from water. Likewise, the transparent sunstone lets different amounts of light through as the sky is scanned, depending on where the sun is hiding.

Unlike the Polynesians, whose most scientific navigation methods were based on knowledge of the stars and their relationship to the seasons and to latitude, the Vikings relied heavily on solar navigation, as polar nights were short in summer, the only time of year when it was reasonably safe or comfortable to go on long sea voyages from places like Norway and Iceland. The sunstone was necessary because, even in summer, the sun was often hidden by full cloud for days on end in that part of the world.

The Vikings also had a symbol or a logo which was as distinctive as the pirates' Jolly Roger of later centuries. This symbol was the raven, carried on a flag or pennant known as the Hrafnsmerki, which literally meant Raven's Mark as in the sense of trademark, although the word *merki* had a broad meaning that included flags and even borders on the map. 'Raven Banner' is the usual English translation nowadays.

Often, though presumably not always, the Raven Banner seems to have had two straight sides and a third side forming a quarter of a circle, creating a larger ground on which to represent the raven than a simple triangle would allow, with tassels flying from the curved side and the two straight sides stiffened with poles at right angles. Thus, the Raven Banner was intended to be as conspicuous as possible even in still air, tassels and all.

The raven was connected to the Norse high god Odin, in the sense that two ravens called Huginn and Munnin continually brought him information. Thus, it bore the totemic power of Odin. Ravens were also notorious for feeding on the corpses of the executed and those slain in battle. As such, the Raven Banner really was the Jolly Roger of its day.

As late as 1066, William the Conqueror's Normans, though they now spoke French, sailed in original-looking Viking longships and flew a version of the Raven Banner, as did the troops of the Norwegian invader Harald Hardrada ('Harold Hard-Advice' or more freely, 'Harold the Hardass'), whom the English under Harold Godwinson defeated at the Battle of Stamford Bridge, only to fall to the Normans at the Battle of Hastings shortly afterward.

All this is depicted in the famous Bayeux Tapestry, from which two scenes are shown on the facing page.

Bayeux Tapestry, Scene 39. Note the Normans' Viking-type longships. Public domain image from the Tapestry shown more fully on the website of Ulrich Harsch at the Hochschule Augsburg, via Wikimedia Commons.

Raven Banner carried by a Norman in the service of William the Conqueror, Bayeux Tapestry. Public domain image via Wikimedia Commons.

To this day, ravens are common in the coats of arms, flags and badges of any place or organisation with some kind of descent from the Norse or Viking world, such as military regiments, units of local government, commemorative organisations, and so on.

As for the Vikings, war and raiding was only one side of their character. In reality, they were farmers to begin with and, in many places that they came to, they eventually settled down and became traders, or farmers once again.

The Vikings sold slaves, and also kept many themselves. It seems that a large and overlooked part of the effort of creating Viking longships was the growing of the wool and the rather monotonous work that was required to make the sails. Viking sheep-farms and sail-making establishments appear to have been operated by slaves, and rather a lot of slaves too.

Viking slaves were often sacrificed to the gods, especially if their master died. On the other hand, mainly because there was no colour bar and plenty of intermarriage, the barrier between master and slave was often porous over time. Slaves who were skilled could rise through the ranks, gain respect, and eventually win freedom, just as in ancient Rome. However, as Andrew Lawler writes in a *National Geographic* article that I cite at the end of this chapter, we can't polish Viking slavery up all that much.

Though it no longer exists in the original sense, the prejudice that linked the consumption of fish to an allegedly backward or low-status way of life, as opposed to respectable people who lived on the proceeds of sheep, beef and dairy farms, survives in the English language in the sense that we say of anything we don't like that it's 'a bit fishy'. Fishy like Gollum in the *Lord of the Rings,* for example.

Fishing was a big industry in Norway by the 1400s. And later on, of course, we discovered the health benefits of cod liver oil and Omega-3s. But in the meantime, the old prejudice against fish seems to have lingered on in Greenland, where it probably also served to uphold a social distinction between Norse and Inuit. Norse Greenland, which could have prospered hugely from fishing but didn't, may thus have ended its days as a backwater clinging to the old, prejudiced ways while the rest of the world moved on, in ways that ultimately contributed to the colony's demise.

There was a similar situation in Iceland, though it didn't actually doom the colony. According to the Icelandic economist Þráinn (Thráinn) Eggertsson, in an article which I also cite at the end of this chapter, while the island's seas and fiords teemed with fish, post-Viking Icelandic society was dominated by its farmers. The Alþingi was dominated by farmers and passed new laws, after the emancipation of the thralls, to force labour to work on farms and not to do other things such as fishing, save on a small and amateur scale.

Farming was a bit less marginal in Iceland than in Greenland, and so the Icelanders managed to survive; though the country stagnated for several centuries, as did its population, which for an equivalent length of time did not greatly exceed fifty thousand. From the late Middle Ages on, other countries fished Icelandic waters on a commercial scale. The main harvesters of the fish were Iceland's more economically developed Norwegian and Danish overlords, of whom the last ruled the island as a dependency until the twentieth century.

Not until the nineteenth century did Iceland get serious about developing its own fishing industry despite the abundance of fish in its waters. By the time that independence came, Iceland had already become more economically diversified, no longer economically in thrall to its farmers, and thus ready for independence.

References

Andrew Lawler, 'Kinder, Gentler Vikings? Not According to Their Slaves', *National Geographic* website, 28 December 2015, URL news.nationalgeographic.com/2015/12/151228-vikings-slaves-thralls-norse-scandinavia-archaeology/

Thráinn Eggertsson, 'No experiments, monumental disasters: Why it took a thousand years to develop a specialized fishing industry in Iceland', *Journal of Economic Behavior and Organization*, Vol. 30, Issue 1, 1996, pp. 1-23.

(There is also a very good entry on the Viking Age in Wikipedia as of the time of writing, and on the Vikings on History.com as well.)

For more, see:

a-maverick.com/blog/vikings-seafarers-who-hated-fish

CHAPTER 5

East past the Icecap, to Djúpivogur

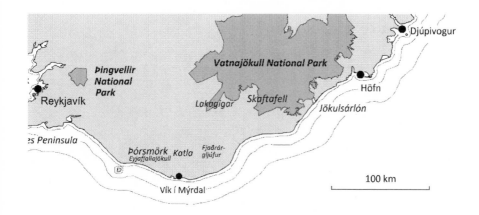

The first stage of my road trip ran from Reykjavik, east to Djúpivogur

MY first stop was a deviation off my route. A short twenty-minute drive to the south of Reykjavík were the Blue Lagoon hot pools. The Blue Lagoon pools are considered by some to be one of the 25 top wonders of the world, though they are not a natural wonder. The Blue Lagoon consists of hot pools in a hardened lava landscape, created by the outflow from a modern geothermal power system.

The water is a milky-blue colour caused by dissolved minerals precipitating out as 'rock flour', as the formerly superheated groundwater cools down during its progress through the machines. Well, I found the Blue Lagoon worse for overcrowding than the Pacific Baths in Rotorua, a

New Zealand tourist destination of similar fame. Even in the off season they were ridiculously busy at the Blue Lagoon!

I parked the car up, got out, went to the reception area, caught glimpses of a crowded pool, and decided against it. I thought, stuff that, I'm not going to get any relaxation time here! I knew there were other outdoor hot pools further north in Mývatn and in other places. So, I decided I would wait until I got to those.

Mývatn is probably the second-most-famous of Iceland's large spas. But as it's in the wild north-east, at the opposite end of the country from Reykjavík and the Golden Triangle, it's much quieter than the Blue Lagoon — which actually has a reputation nowadays for being packed out to the point of 'avoid if possible'. There's almost a kind of snobbery about travel to Iceland, which holds that the Golden Triangle, handy to Reykjavík with all its clubs and bars after a day's sightseeing, is for tourists, while the rest of Iceland is for discerning and intrepid travellers. The sights of the Golden Triangle are still worth seeing. But I can understand how that point of view comes about.

While I was checking out the Blue Lagoon, I came across the Viking World Museum. That was a good find. I changed my plan and went there instead. Inside, I found a replica longboat built by ship maker Gunnar Marel Eggertsson.

Eggertsson started the boat in 1994 and completed it in 1996 using only traditional methods and tools used by the Vikings. I was amazed to see that, in 2000, Eggertsson and a group of Icelandic people went off on a voyage that traced Erik the Red's son Leif Eriksson's journey to

America, stopping off at various countries and islands along the way! Eggertsson's boat is now stored in a specially crafted house so it can be viewed by tourists — like me.

The Ring Road had areas that were only fully safe to drive on for two months of the year, in the height of summer, insofar as the Icelandic summer can be said to have a height. After my unsuccessful trip to the Blue Lagoon hot pools and more successful trip to the Viking World Museum, I finally set out on the Ring Road. It headed northeast up a part of the coast that was known for its mountainous scenery. It was snowing, and I was a bit nervous because in New Zealand, where the winters are mostly quite mild, we normally drive in all-season tyres. If it snows, we need to get out and put chains on. Which is a real drag.

But in Iceland, where people are more used to the cold, they had winter tyres. These turned out to be a dream. Winter tyres made travelling over the icy road easy. When I got back to Queenstown, which is in one of the snowier parts of New Zealand, I made sure to purchase a set to use there.

In Iceland, the Ring Road was fully paved and quite good. But there were a few wow moments when I was suddenly at a one-way bridge or turning into a blind corner. It did remind me of the back roads around the South Island in New Zealand. The road rolled along flat plains that stretched into the distance before colliding with huge snowy mountains and ranges. I did notice that there were not a lot of barriers, so there wasn't much stop you from skidding and heading over the edge. Thank goodness for winter tyres! There are also not a lot of lights along the roadside. I learnt how dark the nights can be in Iceland — like, pitch black!

I do recommend the 112 Iceland and SafeTravel apps, and to manually report where you are as you move around using the green button on 112 Iceland, in addition to making use of the red panic button on 112 Iceland if you need to. So, if you do find yourself in a slippery situation, the right people know where to find you. Just in case!

Iceland is full of walks, treks and hikes — you name it! I wanted to do one that would take me two weeks. But the weather wasn't going to be great, and I realised that it would be safer viewing everything from my car.

I soon learnt how just lucky I was to be in a car, for the shelter it afforded! Not to mention the heater.

Vík í Mýrdal and Thórsmörk

One of the first places I popped into was the picturesque coastal village of Vík, or Vík í Mýrdal, which is not only the southernmost village in Iceland, or on the mainland at any rate, but also the warmest inhabited spot in Iceland.

The village has a history that dates back to Viking times but only became permanently settled in the twentieth century, as there is no harbour. Instead, Vík is a tourist town and road service centre, accessible both to daytrippers from Reykjavík and those pushing on further east.

Vík has black sand beaches that are beautiful to look at but not safe for swimming or even for walking too close to the surf, as they are swept by huge ocean waves and violent currents: there is no land to the south but Antarctica.

The coast at Vík also sports basalt columns (a common sight in Iceland), needle-like rock stacks and a puffin colony. There is a mountain above the village that you can climb, and a spectacular lookout that you can drive up to, as well as waterfalls and other hiking trails in the vicinity.

Unfortunately for Vík, the area is hugely volcanic. The Eyjafjallajökull volcano, which shut down European aviation in 2010, is close nearby, as is the much larger Katla volcano, which last erupted in 1918, before the town was built. Whether Vík will survive the next one is an open question. Vík is the setting for the 2021 TV series *Katla* on Netflix, though as the series is set in the aftermath of an eruption of Katla in which the town is more or less destroyed, it doesn't do Vík's present scenic qualities justice!

This is also the part of Iceland where the notorious eruptions of Lakagígar, the Craters of Laki, took place in 1783 and 1784. You can visit the craters, which are in a finger-like extension of Vatnajökull National Park, the area's national park and Iceland's largest.

Perhaps it is more accurate to say that this volcanism is a two-edged sword today. For it has also created one of the area's greatest tourist attractions, a valley called valley called Þórsmörk, or Thórsmörk.

Þórsmörk is named after the Norse god Thor and means 'Thor's Mark' or 'Thor's Valley': a valley which has Eyjafjallajökull on its southern side. The valley includes hot springs and the wastelands of Landmannalaugar, one of those places you see on the Internet where otherwise barren hills have bright patches of colour and even rainbow-like stripes as though they have been painted.

These colours are created by a volcanic mineral called rhyolite which can display many different tints depending on slight variations in its composition. One eruption may lay down rhyolite of one colour, the next of a different colour, and so on — whence the stripes. And the colours really are bright.

The area is particularly popular over the summer, when the colourful rhyolite is not covered in snow and when the weather is better in any case.

As its name suggests — jökull meaning glacier — the Eyjafjallajökull volcano has a glacier on top, as does the much larger Katla which is at the head of the valley, and a couple of other peaks nearby including one to the north of Þórsmörk, which thus sits nestled between glaciers — really, I think Iceland is a glacier within a glacier: truly the land of ice!

I had wanted to do a five-day trek through Þórsmörk but couldn't because of time constraints. In fact, I was glad I didn't organise to do Þórsmörk in the end, because the road ended up closed the whole time I was there. It was the end of an unusually cold winter when I arrived, and many of the walks that were usually open by now were still shut. People were normally out and about by this time of year, but not yet when I was there.

Beware of Sandstorms!

There is a lot of volcanic sand and ash just lying around everywhere in this area, in ways that contribute to huge volcanic dust storms, sometimes visible from space, as in the following photograph.

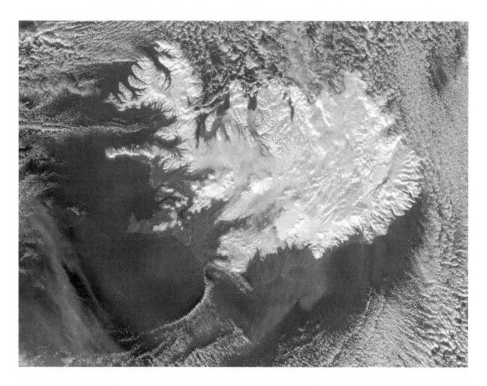

'Dust Storm off Southern Coast of Iceland'. NASA public domain image, photographed on 28 January 2002, via NASA Earth Observatory

As I mentioned in Chapter Two it pays to get Sand and Ash Protection (SAAP) insurance and to follow the wind and weather forecasts carefully as well. You can get volcanic sandstorms elsewhere, but the south is supposed to be the worst.

Until I got caught up in one, I had no proper understanding of the reality of these dust storms and how terrible they could be. I got to Skaftafell at the southern edge of the Vatnajökull National Park, where the winds had picked up dramatically, and I thought "this is great!" That is, until I saw someone else's car windows get blown out. The wind blows all the dust and dry sand across the ground, and you end up with wind blowing in your face, all full of grit and dust.

I spent one night in a tent at Skaftafell waiting for the storm to die down and was woken during the night by another group who just argued for hours over how to put the tent up! I didn't want to risk opening my boot in the ferocious winds, so I left all my gear in the back seat of the car, which was much safer.

I met a woman called Joan who was a teacher from San Diego. She had broken her arm in Oslo and was travelling around in a brand-new car. The winds had picked up and she was too scared to drive. I asked her on earth did she did drive with a broken arm, and she said she changed the gears with her knees. She was on her way back to Reykjavík because of the weather and was cutting her holiday short.

On to Vatnajökull

Next was the Vatnajökull ('Water Glacier') National Park, the biggest park in Iceland, containg Europe's biggest glacier, the Vatnajökull. Much of the National Park is covered by a large ice cap of the Greenlandic type, though much smaller in comparison to Greenland of course. It was stunning. It was all mountains with glaciers and snow-covered everything.

It was such a diverse natural landscape. I noticed few tour buses parked up in places and avoided those.

On the way to Vatnajökull, I went past the spectacular Fjaðrárgljúfur or Feathers Canyon, fjaðrár meaning feathers and gljúfur no doubt related to the English word gulf. This involves a bit of a detour, and unfortunately I missed it.

Sunset at Fjaðrárgljúfur. Photograph by Andrés Nieto Porras, 2 October 2014, CC BY-SA 2.0 via Wikimedia Commons. The photo as posted was very dark, presumably for artistic effect and on a page headed 'Into the Darkness'; I have lightened it to show more of the detail.

There is a very good article about Fjaðrárgljúfur, with more amazing photos, on **guidetoiceland.is**, which also has a page on Vík.

(As you can see, even the gnarliest-looking Icelandic place names such as Fjaðrárgljúfur aren't so difficult to remember, once you learn what their parts mean: parts that are often related to English terms anyway. Thus, if Vík í Mýrdal was in England, it would be called Wick-in-Moordale. And so on.)

Still, I made sure not to miss the Jökulsárlón glacier lagoon on the coast. This is an ice-choked lagoon that lies between the Vatnajökull icecap and the sea. Half the lagoon is in the national park, and half is outside it.

At Jökulsárlón, I got chatting to a few people and it was then I met a kindred soul by the name of Rita. She was travelling in around in a proper off-road SUV while here I was in my Toyota bomb. We exchanged numbers and I would later meet up with her for a coffee with her in her hometown of Brussels. She was lovely. We swapped cameras and took each other's photos in front of the glacier.

Apparently, this was an area where some of the first settlers to Iceland came. It was beautiful: stunning blue water with icebergs floating across the water's surface, occasionally revealing old ice that had its own shades of blue. I stood by the edge of the glacier and breathed in the crisp Arctic air and smelled the rain and stopped to let myself enjoy the peacefulness of the moment.

Everything was a variation on blue: light blue, white with a bluish tinge to it, deep blue and greenish blue. It was just amazing. Then the rain couldn't hold off any longer and began to pour again. That meant I had to get back into the car and carry on. I said goodbye to Rita, for now, and went on my way — places to go and places to see. I warily eyed the darkening skies and the winds started to pick up a bit.

Initially, I had booked two tours online with Icelandic Mountain Guides. I wanted to climb Iceland's highest peak Hvannadalshnjúkur, also spelt Hvannadalshnúkur, which was 2,110 metres high, and to do a glacier walk over the largest glacier in Iceland at Breiðamerkurjökull.

Jökulsárlón, with Rita and 4WD at top

You can imagine my absolute disappointment when the tours were both cancelled because of the weather. Still, I didn't have time to mope, and I didn't have to reschedule. I learned a very good and hard lesson for travel in places like Iceland, or anywhere else that has a fickle, coastal climate, New Zealand included: don't book anything till the day and till you can see the weather yourself. The weather in Iceland is so changeable that it really doesn't pay to be organised!

Anyway, while I was looking into all these different walks all over Iceland, I came to be really impressed by the number of them. There were heaps! You could do tours through deep caves under the ice and snow, and treks up mountains and hillsides. So, I added some of these walks onto my to do list, although I knew I'd be better to wait until the weather fined up!

Trekking is one of the most popular things for tourists to do in Iceland. It's an excellent way to get out and about discovering rich landscapes teeming with wildlife! I'm so glad I didn't just stick to the touristy Golden Triangle, which would have been too busy for me anyway, just like the Blue Lagoon baths.

A Land of Special Horses

Off the beaten track, there are the Icelandic horses and the arctic foxes that live wild, inland from the coast. I saw a few groups of wild horses grazing off to the side of the road as I drove along. That was amazing! I wasn't brave enough to stop and take photos, though.

The Icelandic horse is more of a pony then a horse and used to be called the Icelandic pony, a name that for some reason has gone out of fashion. Icelandic horses/ponies are small and quite stocky. They have five gaits: walk, trot, gallop, 'tölt', and flying pace.

The tölt is a variety of what's called the ambling gait, a medium-speed gait roughly as fast as a trot or a pace, but in which all four legs are moved independently. Ambling is the ideal gait for riding cross-country as it is safe and smooth, and reasonably quick even if it is slower than a gallop.

Trotting and pacing, in which the horses move two legs at once and rock about as a result, are normally used for pulling carriages in harness and not for riding. If you watch harness racing closely, you can see that the horses are moving quite jerkily. Having said that, the Icelandic horse is sometimes ridden at the flying pace.

Some horse breeds amble, others don't. Horses and ponies that amble are often slow gallopers. For that reason, thoroughbreds can't amble. It's in their nature to go flat-out the moment the gates open.

Most breeds of warhorses also had the ability to amble bred out of them. A thunderous cavalry charge was at risk of becoming a lot less thunderous if the horses had the option of deciding that, as they were going cross-country, they should amble for safety's sake!

As people say — there are horses for courses!

One rule they have in Iceland is that no horses can be imported, and horses that are exported can never return. That's because there are no major horse diseases in Iceland, and therefore the animals are healthy and live longer. Norse settlers originally brought ponies to Iceland with them in the 9th and 10th centuries. The Icelandic horse was created out of these.

When the volcano Laki erupted to form the Lakagígar, most of Iceland's horses perished. Conservation efforts were later introduced to build the numbers back up again.

Back on the Road Again

Next, I was driving to Höfn, about three and a half hours north of Jökulsárlón. It was along the Route 1 road and on the way to a town called Egilsstaðir. I noticed a lot of reindeer on the roads around here, and that made my trip quite a bit slower, because I was scared to hit one in my old Toyota. I didn't even know if it had airbags. The reindeer seemed to know when a car was approaching, and to get out of the way, because when they heard me coming, they would hurry off over the road. It was amazing watching them stride across. They were quite fast, and so much bigger in real life than I expected!

I ended up having to find a hostel to stay in at Höfn because the road north to Egilsstaðir was closed. So, I found myself in Höfn for two nights.

I found a guesthouse which I had seen advertised on a sign on the side of the road. Thankfully they had a spare room because the winds were picking up to over 50 knots. They weren't warm either! So, I wasn't keen to try camping again! Höfn is quite a busy tourist area too. It is really close to glaciers and borders the national parks. The main economic activities are fishing and tourism.

My bedroom window in Höfn had a view to die for. The view looked out over four glaciers. There were seals and birds swimming amidst the glacier icebergs, which was strange to me as I had only seen them swimming amidst rocks in New Zealand. I saw a puffin and got close enough to get a quick photo — they were quite hard to spot because their feathers just blended in with the rocks and snow! There are heaps of nesting grounds for the Icelandic puffin all along the coast, quite a tourist attraction themselves. There are also these amazing falcons — gyrfalcons — that can be seen circling in the sky along the coast.

I got up early the next morning to try the road to Egilsstaðir a second time and went to the town's information centre to ask if the road was open. They said they had a snow plough going through soon and if I wanted to get to Egilsstaðir, then I could follow right behind it. I ended up following the snow plough on a completely different road. The car almost got stuck and they told me I could always sleep in the car if it got bad and the road couldn't be cleared.

To top it all off I had a cheap insurance plan that didn't cover damage caused by going out of control on an unsealed or gravel road; that was another reason I didn't want to venture onto the rough roads. I was used to dirt roads in New Zealand, but not here; and I had a crusty old car that did the trick but made me nervous. There were actually a few gravel stretches on the roads I did take, and that slowed me down again.

I was not going to race around: in fact, I mostly stayed well below the speed limit of 80 kilometres per hour. It was nice, though. I got to just take my time and enjoy the scenery along the way. There were also some areas where I hit fog, and that made it quite hard to see anything. There were huge power pylons beside the road. They emerged from the fog looking ominous: big dark shapes looming into the distance.

The weather seemed to clear the closer I got to Egilsstaðir, and I began to see a different kind of scenery sweep past my window.

The landscape was very rocky, and instead of grass there was a sort of green moss covering the ground in tufts. Small areas had patches of what I thought was an alpine grass. There were dark tunnels under the hillsides that always gave me a bit of thrill to go through. There were places where it was just a sea of blue flowers, which was such a stark contrast to the foggier rock areas and white snow. It made it all the prettier, though apparently this were an invasive weed called Nootka Lupin or Alaskan Lupin.

The plant was introduced in 1945 to combat soil erosion and brought nitrogen into the soil for fertility. It has since spread across most of Iceland and people can't seem to decide whether it's a good or a bad thing. I thought it was pretty!

(We've got a similarly colourful species called the Russell Lupin growing wild in similar mountain terrain in the South Island of New Zealand. As in Iceland, somebody thought it would be a good idea to introduce it to boost fertility, and then it got away from them. Vistas of pink, blue and purple lupins in flower with a mountain lake and a snowy peak in the background are now among the most iconic tourism images of New Zealand, even though the Russell Lupin is quite harmful to New Zealand wilderness ecology and is now classed as a weed. So, it's interesting to see that Iceland and the South Island of New Zealand both have this identical issue. The Russell Lupin in New Zealand is said to be 'beloved by tourists and hated by environmentalists': and it sounds like the situation with the Nootka Lupin in Iceland is the same.)

I was told the East Coast of Iceland has more ancient rocks then in the west. And I was also aware that the summer season, when the small country gets overrun with something like 1.7 million tourists, was fast approaching!

Along the way, there were pockets of warmth and steam because of Iceland's geothermal activity. The whole of Iceland runs on natural power sources, so heating was cheap and unlimited. Alongside the geothermal energy resource are the hydroelectric stations, which generate most of Iceland's power. I thought well, why not.

They have these fantastic resources that are all natural and part of the environment, which can be harnessed and used for the benefit of the people living there! Iceland was on the expensive side too, and so I thought that it was good to get some savings on something, so that they didn't end up with the same degree of unemployment and poverty as in parts of Greenland.

As I drove further up the coast the Ring Road wove around mountains that dropped into the sea. It was amazing to look out over the ocean as I drove. It was right there! The sea was rough, and waves splashed up the sides below. I got to a place that was about halfway between Höfn and Egilsstaðir called Djúpivogur, at the end of a peninsula next to a fiord called Berufjörður.

Djúpivogur pier with egg sculptures

Djúpivogur was just a small smattering of houses and was originally a Danish trading post. It was a slight deviation off the main road, but I needed the break. There was a huge outdoor sculpture I heard was worth stopping at. It was just to the north of the small town and so I parked my car up and went wandering around for a bit. The sculpture was quite a well-known one and consisted of all these eggs atop stone columns. They were quite neat and represented 34 different types of nesting birds in

Iceland. The sculpture was called Eggin í Gleðivík, created by the artist Sigurður Guðmundsson in 2009.

Eggin í Gleðivík means the eggs of Merry Bay. Eggin is practically the same as eggs, or the eggs, in English while gleð, meaning merry, looks like the English world glad. As I say, Icelandic placenames really aren't as tricky as you might think at first.

I was surprised at how modern the town of Djúpivogur was. And there were rows of newly planted trees around the town, which made it feel more homely.

The backdrop to Djúpivogur was really pretty. A huge, pyramid-shaped mountain was the central feature of the horizon, and on either side of this mountain there were yet another two glaciers. I found out that the pyramid-like mountain was called Búlandstindur. Like many other sorts of pyramids, Búlandstindur is said to harbour supernatural powers. And to judge from a photo that appears overleaf, you can see why people might have thought that way.

One thing about Iceland is all the mountains: while not very high, they are spectacular nonetheless!

Even though the weather was terribly cold, Iceland just comes alive through the magical landscapes and the natural raw beauty, whether it be rain or shine (or blizzards).

There is something about the stunning natural setting of Iceland: no matter the weather, it brings out different elements of everything. On a cloudy day the sea becomes a dark haunting grey, and then on a sunny day the sea shines with blue and green and grey all swirled into one. The water sliding off moss covered rocks in the rain gives the moss a completely different beauty than on a sunny day.

Búlandstindur as seen from Djúpivogur. Photograph by Elísabet Guðmundsdóttir, May 2006, http://djupivogur.is; CC-BY-SA 3.0 via Wikimedia Commons.

I think that the only way to find the best-kept secrets of Iceland, or any country for that matter, is to head to the smaller towns; to the rough-edged backroads and twisted mountain paths that wind their way through incredible settings.

For more, see:

a-maverick.com/blog/east-past-the-icecap-to-djupivogur

CHAPTER 6

Burnt Njáll and the Valkyries: Tales from the Icelandic Sagas

THE sagas are great epic poems that tell the history of Viking communities in ways that vary from the factual to the fanciful. The word saga means 'saying', in the sense of oral history. They're written down now, of course, and indeed they have been since the Middle Ages. They are often called the Icelandic Sagas, as Iceland was where they were written down. And just as well, as they were forgotten everywhere else, though the experts are sure that most of them were told all over the Norse realm.

There is often a moral to the sagas. In Njáls Saga (there's only one 'l' in the Norse possessive), the main issues concern a touchy kind of masculinity. Njáll is teased by the other Vikings because he can't grow a proper beard, while another Viking called Flosi is insulted when given a well-intended gift of a silk cloak, as he considers this to be effeminate. Njáll and Flosi try to prove that they are tough, but in doing so they unleash all kinds of mayhem, with the result that half-way through the story Njáll is burnt alive along with most of his family in a house-fire lit by his enemy Flosi. This is then avenged by Burnt Njáll's surviving relatives. Eventually, after about fifty years, the vendetta peters out with everyone agreeing that all that offence taken about not being able to grow a proper beard and a gift of allegedly girly clothing was a bit silly, really.

93

Arthur Rackham, The Ride of the Valkyries, *1910*

Public domain image via Wikimedia Commons

Meanwhile, there are stories within stories. The Valkyries, which we associate with the German composer Richard Wagner's Opera *Die*

Walküre (The Valkyries) and its musical highlight The Ride of the Valkyries, are an authentic part of Norse mythology. Their name means 'choosers of the slain' and the idea that they bear brave warriors off to Valhalla is only one aspect of their being. For also, they are like the fates in Greek mythology, actually deciding who is to be destroyed. In one section of Njáls Saga, which is actually a very complicated story, twelve Valkyries are described as weaving the fate of those about to be slain at the forthcoming battle of Clontarf, in Ireland. The Valkyries use intestines for thread, severed heads for weights, and swords and spears as weaving-implements.

Perhaps, as with the Greeks, there is an element here of 'those whom the gods wish to destroy, they first make mad', so that the squabbling men unwitting fulfil a destiny woven by the Valkyries up above.

The English artist Arthur Rackham's engraving, above, makes the Valkyries appear rather less as innocuous retrievers of the slain, bound for glory, and rather more as if they are the horsewomen of the apocalypse.

Lastly, Njáll's another cognate: it's Norse for Neil. Imagine a Viking named Neil. It seems an oddly harmless sounding name, for a Viking.

For more, see:

a-maverick.com/blog/burnt-njall-valkyries-icelandic-sagas

CHAPTER 7

The Northeast and the Dark Castles

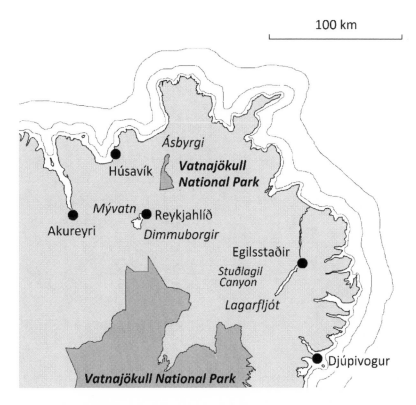

Northeast Iceland, from Djúpivoigur to Akureyri

FTER Djúpivogur, the roads formed something of a network. But
there were basically two main options for getting to Egilsstaðir; one
that went inland, and another that hugged the rugged coastline. The
beaches below were covered in ink-black sand bordered by high rocky
cliffs. I felt I had seen enough of the coast to warrant following an inland

route. This turned out to be partly a gravel road. I crossed over vast expanses of water, and in places the road was so narrow there was only enough room for one car. I was lucky I didn't meet any other oncoming traffic. In some places the mist was thick and then it would disappear and instead cover the tops of mountains and hills. There were plenty of potholes filled with water along the gravel road, too, so it was just as well I was already going slowly in any case.

I loved how dramatic the landscape was: all twisted into rocky mountains, and with snow-covered shrubs and moss instead of grass. It was very mountainous along the way to Egilsstaðir; it looked like someone had just pinched the earth together.

At several spots along the way, I saw an Icelandic horse tethered to a post and grazing along the side of the road. It was very windy in parts and there was just the odd house here and there. I drove past lakes, past rocky areas with splats of ice and snow, then through areas that were covered in more green tufts of moss. Then there were parts that honestly made me think for a moment that I was driving through New Zealand.

After an hour and forty minutes I got to Egilsstaðir. That was how long it took, even though Egilsstaðir is only about eighty kilometres from Djúpivogur by the shortest route.

Egilsstaðir was a town founded in 1947, when the local farmers realised that they needed a town to service their needs. This makes it fairly modern and new compared to other places. Still, with a population of more than two thousand permanent residents, it was quite well established and very pretty. There were shops, and the streets were filled with people out and about. It was incredible to drive through barren landscapes where you saw nobody and to then arrive here and see Egilsstaðir full of life and teeming with tourists.

The very oldest house in the town was only built in 1944, yet it has already become a bit of a tourist attraction. Lots of towns and suburbs, in places like New Zealand or America, have a founder's house that's called the Old Homestead or something like that. Well, in Egilsstaðir, they've got the not-so-old Homestead!

Adding to Egilsstaðir's allure was the fact it sat on the banks of the lengthy Lagarfljót lake. Within the lake there is a creature that is like the Icelandic version of the Loch Ness monster. It's called the Lagarfljót worm or the Iceland worm monster – first mentioned, as far as we know, in Icelandic folklore from the 1300s. It's supposed to be a snake-like creature that occasionally emerges from the murky depths and can be as long as a bus – safe to say I never saw one. But there are plenty of locals who claim to have seen it. An interesting tale!

A 1585 map of Iceland by Abraham Ortelius includes a Latin inscription beside the Lagarfljót lake, to the effect that it contains a serpent of monstrous proportions which is a menace to the inhabitants and comes out when something important is about to happen. Spot the struggling polar bears as well! The relevant part of the map is shown on the next page.

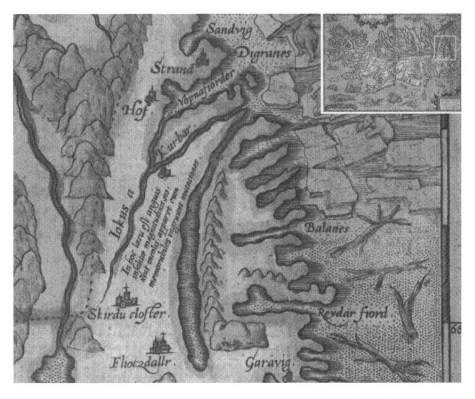

Excerpt from Abraham Ortelius's map of Iceland (Island Theatrum Orbis Terrarum Ortelius), *1585, with location inset, showing the Lagarfljót and a Latin note about its monster*

Wikimedia Commons montage by Josef Moser, CC BY-SA 4.0

A new attraction in this area, west of the Lagarfljót lake, is the Stuðlagil Canyon, in which the river Jökulsá, or Jökla, flows between basalt columns that rise dramatically on both sides. The river through the canyon used to be very deep, swift and turbid, until the taking of part of its flow for hydroelectric power in 2009 permanently lowered its level by seven or eight metres. This revealed more of the columns and also made the canyon more accessible to visitors. The usual colour of the water in the canyon changed from brown to blue as well. This is perhaps one of the few cases where hydro works have resulted in some natural wonder being revealed, as opposed to being submerged!

There are lots of amazing canyons in Iceland, by the way — like Fjaðrárgljúfur, further back toward Vík, Stuðlagil is just one of them!

I spent the night in a hostel, and then carried on the next morning to my next stop, Húsavík, which was further two-and-a-half-hour drive according to the road maps and guidebooks. Although, it took me longer as I stopped constantly, snapping photos and just staring out at the icy land.

I drove past the beautiful shallow inland lake and thermal spa called Mývatn. I would double back to visit it to the next day. Though coastal in most places, Route One turns inland in this part of Iceland to go past Mývatn, surrendering the coast to a local coast road called Route 85. I had the choice of getting to Húsavík by way of Route 85, but that road was just too circuitous. And I'd seen plenty of coast anyway, which was why I had already taken the rough inland road to Egilsstaðir.

This time round, the inland road was going to be the better one. All the same, I planned to then scoot northward to the coast and spend a night in Húsavík, the first town on my itinerary that was actually on the northern coast of Iceland, facing the North Pole.

Húsavík means bay of houses. It's thought that it may be the first place where actual houses were built in Iceland, sometime around 870 CE, though Reykjavík is said to be the first completely permanent settlement.

A more recent claim to fame is that the Apollo astronauts did some of their training in the vicinity of Húsavík, in a patch of volcanic desert that scientists thought to be more like the surface of the moon than almost anywhere else that was easily accessible to the astronauts, though they trained at various barren locations in the USA as well. The Apollo 15 astronaut Al Worden called the wilds outside Húsavík "a place so stark and barren I felt as if I were already on the moon."

Driving to Húsavík was amazing. It snowed, there was sleet and then there was wind. You name it, I saw it.

An aerial panorama of Húsavík

Wikimedia Commons image (2017) by Chensiyuan, CC-BY-SA 4.0

Húsavík was very small and compact, with a population of about two thousand once again. I could see that tourism made up for a lot of its income – everything was related to tourists. It sits tucked in around Skjálfandi Bay and offers whale watching tours. In fact, the town claims to be the capital of Icelandic whale watching (that is, as opposed to Icelandic whaling).

I found this great church from the early 1900's, Húsavíkurkirkja. The church had a high forest green steeple and looks down toward the bay. I stayed in a hostel with views over the bay that night: it was so cosy.

I went to the Turf House Museum, also known as the Culture House, which was about twenty kilometres out from Húsavík in the direction of Akureyri, in a village called Grenjaðarstaður.

Gosh, was that interesting! It reminded me of the hobbit houses in Matamata, New Zealand, that were the abode of the Hobbits in Peter Jackson's *Lord of the Rings* movies. Turf houses used to be found all over Iceland in the past, and the more I read and saw, the more I understood why!

The houses are built from stone and wood (when available) and then covered in moss and grass on top – truly a 'green' house. It was interesting, because I had heard of the same style of houses being built in other parts of Scandinavia, most especially in Norway. The Norse brought the style to Iceland. They are called 'sod roofs', and it is considered a traditional Scandinavian style.

In Norway the homes were built of logs and the roof was covered in soil and grass to stop it blowing away in the strong winds and after seeing that all for myself it made complete sense!

A traditional turf house on the Shetlands. The Icelandic ones were similar.

They had teacups on display at the Turf House Museum, and this incredible ring made from wires all plaited together to make an engagement band. It was fitted with a piece of metal that had a little coloured gem in the centre. It was quite amazing, and I had never seen anything quite like it before! It seemed the more of Iceland I saw, and the more I discovered and learned, the more intricate and unique I found the culture! It was a solid, distinct culture that I really did admire.

The sod houses stood in rows, cutting down on the need for walls and on the heating requirement, which would have been greater if they were separate. Rocks walls separated them and on top were the sod roofs. In Iceland, a lot of the houses had sod walls as well. Some of the interiors

104

like the cooking house had stone walls – which surprised me because I thought that would have made the room too cold – but I suppose when the stones heat up, they hold the heat longer than wood. That would have been magical in winter!

It was a very odd experience wandering around these homes. They didn't smell damp but very earthy and weren't as dark as I thought they would have been.

In finding out about the turf houses, I was surprised to learn that there was actually a farm in the western part of the island that is said to have been Erik the Red's. I made a note to stop there when I got over to that part of Iceland.

I spent the night in this little guest house called Árból, which only cost me about US $100 a night. It was a historic house which just added to all the excitement of being in Iceland. It wasn't super old, but it was one of the older ones in the area, built in 1903. The owner was extremely nice and gave me plenty of information about the area and what to see and do. He told me all about the hot pools in the area, and I decided I would check those out the following day. I did have to share a bathroom, but that didn't bother me because there were only a couple of other people spending the night there at the same time I was. It had a very cosy feel about it, and the bed was comfortable!

I went out the next day in my car. It was an easy forty-minute drive around a headland and back inland towards Ásbyrgi, a large and sheltered canyon containing a forest of birch and willow, which looked so green and lush compared to the rocky landscape above it.

This was the spot that I showed a photograph of in Chapter One. Here is a photo of the head of the valley, which is horseshoe-shaped with a pit, called the Botnstjörn Pond, under the horseshoe. There is a bit of greenery on view in this photo, taken in late May, but not as much as in the photo in Chapter One, which was taken in late July.

'Aerial View of Ásbyrgi'. Photo by Hansueli Krapf, 21 May 2008, CC BY-SA 3.0 via Wikimedia Commons.

I was there even earlier in spring, just before the movable date in late April when the Icelanders celebrate the first day of summer under the old Norse calendar. So, I was fortunate to see any greenery at all.

Ásbyrgi means 'shelter of the gods'. In Norse mythology it was created by the hoofprint of Odin's eight-legged horse Sleipnir. A more scientific view is that it was formed by a huge, temporary waterfall bursting out from melting glaciers, which scoured Ásbyrgi out from the surrounding plateau and presumably also formed the Botnstjörn, where the waters must have fallen with greatest force. In many places the walls are about a hundred metres high, that is, more than three hundred feet. Where would that flood have stood on the kayaking scale, I wonder?

Back in Húsavík, I visited the Húsavík hot pools. I was told there was a small geothermal lake just to the south of Húsavík, which was another popular spot in which to relax, but I didn't go there.

Hot pools and springs are a big deal in Iceland – one the most popular activities. The enjoyment of bathing in the geothermal hot pools and springs, dates right back to the time of the Vikings. I thought then what a pity it wasn't the right time of year for the jaw-dropping display of the Northern Lights, imagine sitting in a Viking age hot pool watching the panoramic display light up the sky. Now, that would have been awesome!

The hot pools I ended up at were not a natural geothermal formation; they were artificial pools fed from pipes driven into the ground at a campsite. I had a quick soak and decided it was time to move on. I was headed to Mývatn next. I had heard that the Mývatn spa was temporarily closed for maintenance at that time. But that wasn't a problem for me, even though I had hoped to visit them earlier on. I was in the land of natural hot springs, so surely, I would finally get to one in my travels. Meanwhile, there were plenty of other things to do and see at Mývatn.

I packed up the car and headed off along the route to Mývatn. Mývatn is one of the most beautiful lakes in the world. It is a shallow lake full of clear water, with a flat bottom and a maximum depth of only 4.5 metres. Within it sit tiny islands covered in greenery, in stark contrast to the usual rocky landscapes of Iceland. Everywhere you can see the bottom and the algae growing on the bottom, and how the islands rise up from the bottom, often quite abruptly like rocks.

The name Mývatn means Midgewater, or Midge Lake. The midges apparently get very bad here. I had experienced them in their dreaded swarms when I was hiking in Scotland!

There were several walking trails at Mývatn, and I wanted to do some of them that day. I had to drive to a small town called Reykjahlíð and walk to the areas I wanted to visit. You could drive to some of the lakeside attractions, but I saw that the road was in three digits, so I wasn't going to attempt it.

Mývatn, when I was there

Mývatn in better weather

I walked, first, to a place called Dimmuborgir which was known for its unusual landscapes. There were rock pillars and tube-shaped formations. These accounted for the name Dimmuborgir, which meant 'dark castles' – very fitting I thought.

Dimmuborgir Paths Sign

Dimmuborgir, 'The Dark Castles'
Most touristy photos of this area are taken in better weather, when the area
doesn't look nearly so grim and dim. This is the real deal!

More Dimmuborgir Landscape

It was bitterly cold, and I was dressed in all my winter get-up, which paradoxically meant that I soon got too hot from all the exercise. I decided to take it easy and walk at a slower pace. The place was well sign-posted and I was relieved to find that all the signs and information panels had an English text alongside the Icelandic. I came across one panel that was about figures from local folklore called the Yule Lads.

Dimmuborgir Sign, describing the Yule Lads

The Yule Lads are little dwarf-like men that are said, in folklore, to live in the area. They are a band of thirteen brothers who have now become associated with Christmas in Iceland. A more modern tradition is for children to leave a shoe on their windowsills thirteen days prior to Christmas and depending on their behaviour the Yule Lads will place a rotten potato if they are bad or a small treat if they have been good. I thought it was brilliant little tradition and one I had never heard of before I stumbled across the signpost. That was also the first I'd heard of the Yule Lads themselves. I later went and looked them and was in fits of laughter as I read the English translations of the Icelandic names; stubby, spoon-licker, door-slammer, candle-stealer and doorway sniffer were just some of the thirteen! They are funny.

On a more serious note, though, Icelandic people are quite in tune with traditional folklore and people still tell their kids these stories today. They tell of mythical elves and trolls who live in stones, and construction workers have even avoided areas because mythical beings are supposed to live there too. In Norse mythology elves come in the light-side and the dark-side versions, that is, good ones and evil ones. I was amazed to discover after my walk that elves, trolls and such beings seemed so incorporated into the local culture still. I found it all quite intriguing and really wanted to find out more about it all when I had the time!

I managed to get one more walk in for the day and that was to the exquisite Grjótagjá lava cave. The route there was busy, and a few other people were walking to it as well. It used to be a popular bathing spot, but now people aren't allowed into the water because, after a 1975 eruption, the water temperature rose to over 50 degrees Celsius in places. This created a risk that people would be scalded as they moved around. It was a neat place to see, though, and I heard that it was also a film site for some scenes in the *Game of Thrones* TV series. A bathing sequence was spliced in to make it look like actors were bathing in the Grjótagjá lava cave's pool, when of course they weren't. The whole walking day took around seven hours and left me quite tired.

I returned to my base at Reykjahlíð, which was quite a hilly area and quite green too. It sits on the shores of Mývatn and only has 300 permanent residents. A volcanic eruption from the nearby Krafla volcano, called the 'Mývatn Fires', destroyed the original village by means of a lava flow and associated fires in 1729. The lava stopped short of the church, supposedly because of the prayers of the village priest. The church was rebuilt in 1972, so nothing much now remains of the old village. The nearby Krafla volcano still has eruptions every now and then.

I found a place called Hlíð Cottages that sit up on the hill behind Reykjahlíð with views to Lake Mývatn below. I had a cottage to myself, and it was lovely to retreat to after a day out walking. Incidentally, you can treat ð as a d for the purposes of Internet searches; Hlid Cottages will get you there!

The following day I decided to set out on another walk, so I drove about 8 km and parked up. I found the Krafla Caldera, a collapsed volcanic area with a stunning crater. I was a bit worried about walking there on my own, so I brought an Icelandic SIM card. I always buy a SIM card for whatever country I am in; among other things, it saves on the costs of global roaming. I had learnt my lesson when I visited India the year before and clocked up a NZ $2,000 phone bill – I wasn't pleased, obviously.

I got back to my accommodation quite late and was popping out to the supermarket in the dark when I found my car had got stuck in the snow. Luckily, the guy who was working on renovating a building helped me out.

I ended up at a bar and got talking with some of the locals. I asked them about the Yule Lads, and they told me, very seriously, that they were real and lived in a cave nearby. I told them that one of the caves I had walked by did look like someone was living in it. I said that I had got spooked and left without taking any photos. They all burst out laughing and told me it was a local joke they played on tourists! The joke got me even more interested in the folk tales, though, and that's when I found out about more of the revival in Norse mythology.

The following day was the first day of summer... and it snowed! Heading toward the West Coast of Iceland was exciting. After a short drive I found myself in Akureyri, a city dubbed the capital of the north and the second most populous urban area in Iceland after Reykjavík. It was a beautiful place, and also a busy fishing port. It was here that I tried the dish called skyr, a milk-cultured product that was brought to Iceland 1,100 years ago by the Norse. It was like yogurt topped with sugar, but with a milder and less acid flavour than most kinds of yogurt. I've seen it since in the supermarket back in New Zealand. Other traditional foods I had heard that were still quite popular (unlike the fermented shark) were boiled sheep's heads, fluffy pastries, and fish.

Reference

The quote from Al Worden comes from his book (with Francis French), *Falling to Earth: An Apollo 15 Astronaut's Journey to the Moon,* Washington DC, Smithsonian Books, 2011, at p. 118.

For more, see:

a-maverick.com/blog/northeast-and-dark-castles

CHAPTER 8

The Lord of the Rings and Narnia (original version)

A STRANGE and goggle-eyed dwarf named Andvari, which means the wary (vari) or watchful one, lived under a waterfall, where he guarded a soggy hoard of gold. Andvari had the power to turn himself into a pike, a fast, predatory fish, at will, and this is how he subsisted for food. He was always eating fish, while watching out with exaggerated wariness for anyone who might rob him of his hoard, one precious part of it in particular.

For the Vikings (for whom fish was the food of thralls) the fearfulness and fishiness of Andvari probably made him seem like a fallen and wretched creature; and probably also rather comical as well.

Andvari is, of course, the inspiration for J. R. R. Tolkien's Gollum. In fact, for all practical purposes he *is* Gollum.

In the original Viking tale, Andvari's hoard attracted the attention of the foolish god Loki, who made Andvari hand over his gold. Loki noticed that Andvari was reluctant to hand over one last treasure, a ring called Andvaranaut – which I will call the Ring, since we know that that's what it's all about – and so Loki insisted that Andvari give him the Ring as well. Andvari said that the Ring was a special ring that could be used to produce more gold. The dwarf urged Loki to let him keep the Ring and make more gold for himself so that both would be satisfied.

Loki, of course, didn't listen (he never did) and made off with the Ring, leaving Andvari to curse it so that it would bring misfortune to everyone who possessed it.

The Ring passes through a succession of hands, bringing doom and disaster to all. Along the way, one of its possessors turns into a dragon, guarding the ring and the treasure generated from it, until the dragon is slain by a hero called Sigurd (to the Norse) or Siegfried (to the Germans).

Like Aragorn in *The Lord of the Rings,* Sigurd/Siegfried kills the dragon with a sword re-forged from the shards of his father's sword.

For the tale of Andvari's Ring is indeed the forerunner of J. R. R. Tolkien's *Lord of the Rings* and *The Hobbit.* It is also the inspiration for the German composer Richard Wagner's famous *Ring* cycle of operas: *Das Rheingold* (in which the golden hoard is fished out of the Rhine); *Die Walküre* (the Valkyries); *Siegfried* (about the hero); and *Götterdämmerung,* the Twilight of the Gods, in which it seems that everyone who has tried on the Ring gets their comeuppance. One Ring, in other words, to rule them all, in Tolkien and Wagner alike.

It is the Ring that brings on Ragnarök, as well.

In the pre-Tolkien versions of the tale, the downfall of the Ring-bearers also includes Sigurd / Siegfried. For, it turns out that Siegfried is not as good at resisting the temptations of power-madness as Tolkien's unassuming Hobbits, who basically resist power from the outset. There were no Hobbits in the tale before Tolkien came along. And so, before Tolkien, even the hero goes over to the dark side of the force in ways that hasten the world to its destruction.

Out of the ashes of a fallen world in which *nobody* could resist the lure of the Ring, a better world might be born. But that's the nearest the story gets to a happy ending.

Notoriously, the Nazis loved the Wagner version (he *was* Hitler's favourite composer, after all). But with the obtuseness of the character played by Kevin Kline in *A Fish Called Wanda,* the Nazis failed to grasp that the tale was being told of them too. Either that, or they had a bit of a death-wish. Probably, both.

For the Ring is all about power-madness and a cataclysm in which the power-mad will go down like James Cagney in *White Heat* ("Made it ma! Top of the world."). Or Hitler as played by Bruno Ganz in *Der Untergang* (Downfall), the film that spawned a million spoofs.

These days, we might wonder whether the Ring we can no longer take off signifies addiction to fossil fuels followed by another form of doom in fire and ice. Or, nuclear weapons, which nobody in possession of them wants to give up but which will inevitably be (re-)used sooner or later if they don't give them up. Perhaps the Ring that must either be destroyed or used wisely is not made of gold, but uranium.

Or, then again, the Ring might also warn us about abstract financial greed of the kind that today jacks up house prices till the city becomes uninhabitable for the workers, thus killing the goose that lays the economy's golden eggs.

It's interesting how many tales there are of this sort, including stories of grindstones that produce too much and cause havoc, flooding the world with their product. I'm going to mention one of those tales a bit later on. Likewise, many have heard of the mythically accursed King Midas of Ancient Greece whose touch turned everything into gold, including his food and his daughter. All these tales seem to preach that if people can somehow learn to live in a more moderate and less greedy sort of a way, there will be fewer problems in the world.

For otherwise, as a powerful 1960s protest song has it, we will be condemned to live on the Eve of Destruction. An eve, which the Viking and Wagner versions of the story treat as the eve of *inevitable* destruction.

Tolkien would have regarded the original Viking version, and the Wagnerian one too, as overly fatalistic. Fatalism was a common criticism of 'pagans' from the Christian point of view, which was certainly also Tolkien's point of view, similar to that of his friend C. S. Lewis though less tub-thumping. Both Tolkien and Lewis were experts on Norse mythology, which they sought to weave into their own tales, of hobbits in Tolkien's case and Narnia in that of Lewis.

Like the sharp-faced commissar in front Bob Hoskins's Nikita Khrushchev in *Enemy at the Gates,* Jesus's message was interpreted by people such as Lewis and Tolkien as one of 'give them hope'; the hope being partly to do with the idea of a world in which evil and stupidity don't always have to triumph, or to wreck everything, in the end.

Christian hope was probably quite down-to-earth to begin with, though after the fall of the Western Roman Empire Christianity also became pessimistic about the everyday world, which the Vikings called Middle-Earth, between Heaven and Hell which they also believed in in their own way. However, the defeat of the Nazis would have lent credence to a more redemptive view of the everyday world – Middle-Earth – when Tolkien was penning his works, *The Lord of the Rings* in particular.

And so, Tolkien delivers a happy ending that wasn't noticeable before. And he achieves this by injecting a saviour who is a voice of reason and moderation, someone wise enough to break the cycle of madness leading to the world's otherwise inevitable destruction. The saviour is a collective one, centring on the hobbits and the wise wizard Gandalf.

Viking culture is not quite dead, even now. For instance – what do I really mean when I say, "I was unscathed"? One answer is that a spear of misfortune flung by the goddess Skaði missed me. Skaði goes about on skis in a land that is always winter, tossing her spears of misfortune from this realm into the mortals of Middle-Earth.

Skaði's gig is *Schadenfreude,* a German word that is cognate with her name, as are the Scandinavian and German words for damage and, of course, our own word 'scathe'

Only Loki, the foolish god, ever succeeded in making Skaði laugh, and only once.

Skaði seems to be a relative of the Greek goddess Diana the Hunter, perhaps even of the fearsome Indian goddess Kali. Of course, in neither of those sunny climes does a land of perpetual winter feature prominently in local myth. For the Norse, Skaði is not only a Diana or Kali-like figure but also the goddess of winter and mountains, and of everything cold and sharp in general.

'Skaði hunting in the mountains'

Public domain image by 'H.L.M.', in Mary H. Foster, *Asgard Stories: Tales from Norse Mythology,* Silver, Burdett & co., 1901, p. 79.

If the Ring of Andvari is the original version of *The Lord the Rings,* Skaði's frozen realm is – you guessed it – Narnia.

For more, see:

a-maverick.com/blog/lord-of-the-rings-and-narnia-original

CHAPTER 9

Erik the Red's Homestead

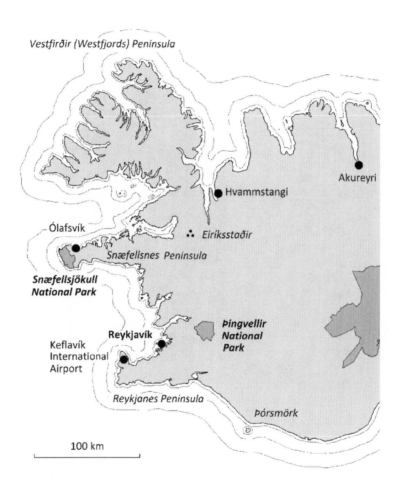

West Iceland, including Eiríksstaðir

AS I recall, I had been driving for almost eight days now, stopping off here and there and staying wherever I pleased. I thought that I could have quite easily spent three weeks in Iceland just sightseeing and hiking. I ended up going through a blizzard somewhere after Akureyri, and that really tested my driving skills and confidence.

Reconstructed Viking Longhouse at Eiríksstaðir

I made my way down the western coast, bypassing the hand-shaped Westfjords Peninsula (which is worth another visit), and dropped in to the Selasetur Íslands, the Icelandic Seal Centre in Hvammstangi, a big red barn-like building that houses a natural history museum and research centre entirely devoted to seals!

Everybody talks about saving the whales; but many species of seal were hunted almost to extinction as well, for their meat, their blubber (made into oil), and for the thick waterproof fur that some species have. Breathable but water-repellent, seal fur was very fashionable for outdoor attire at one time; it was the nearest thing our Victorian forebears had to Gore-Tex. All in all, about the only difference between commercial sealing and commercial whaling was that it took more seals to yield the same profit as one whale. Yet the poor old seals aren't in the forefront of our conservation consciousness to the same degree. The Seal Centre strives to change that.

A short distance later, I made it to Eiríksstaðir: an open-air museum on the site of what is scientifically believed to be the actual homestead of Erik the Red, the founder of Greenland.

His son Leif, founder of a short-lived Viking settlement in Canada, was also born here at the homestead. There were some areas where investigators found remains of houses and buildings, and the open-air museum included replicas of them all. They all had the sod roofs above them. The views over the ocean were amazing even if the weather was starting to turn a bit sour. There were people greeting tourists dressed in traditional clothing and there were Icelandic horses tethered outside of the houses. It was a fantastic archaeological site and one that I thoroughly enjoyed and was glad I made a point to stop there.

Icelandic West Coast

*The Olafsvik area on the Snæfellsnes Peninsula, with
national park maps and signs*

I was on a road that either led back to Route One or continued on to
the Snæfellsnes Peninsula, another place I decided to visit on the spur of

the moment. I drove as far as a place called Ólafsvík on the Snæfellsnes Peninsula. Ólafsvík used to be a major commercial port serving Denmark, but it is not so important as a port these days. The weather was vile. I had a quick look at the coastline, which was all rocks and rough waves. I saw the Snæfellsjökull, a 700,000-year-old glacier that sits on the Peninsula and also is part of the Snæfellsjökull National Park.

Axlar-Björn

One of the signs concerned a local villain called Björn Pétursson, nicknamed Axlar-Björn, which literally means Shoulder-Bear, who murdered travellers on the Snæfellsnes Peninsula in the 1500s. Rumour has it that Axlar-Björn's curiously growing collection of overland ponies made people suspicious. Well, that's one version of the story, anyway.

A local person I met in a café alerted me to the Landbrotalaug hot pools nearby, so I set out to find them and finally got my taste of real outdoor Icelandic hot springs! They weren't easy to find and in fact I can't even give you directions because I can't remember how I found them. All I know is that they ended up being a bit of a mission! Well worth going to though; no one else was there at the time so in I got! I decided it was probably about time to head back to Reykjavík. I had one more night left before I had to return my car and catch my flight out of Iceland in the evening.

So, I headed back and booked into another hotel where I slept like a log! Then I packed my things into my backpack, then took the car back to SADcar rentals and got a shuttle to Keflavík International Airport.

I was glad to have visited before peak tourist season – there were still plenty of tourists around on my journey and I'd hate to imagine what it was like with 1.7 million tourists cramming in.

But before I conclude, I must tell one more Viking tale!

For more, see:

a-maverick.com/blog/erik-the-reds-homestead

CHAPTER 10

The Twilight of the Gods (the tale of fire and ice)

THE Vikings had a constant sense of foreboding, whereby the violent tendencies of their society might destroy the world. The only thing that prevented this from happening was the limited power of their weapons, which – so far – only consisted of things like swords and shields. But the gods, with greater powers, would gradually fall to fighting among themselves in a similar spirt, and this would doom the world as the gods had greater powers. The world would ultimately be destroyed in a great battle called Ragnarök, meaning the fate or twilight of the ruling powers (regin). This was constantly prophesied:

—an axe age, a sword age
—shields are riven—
a wind age, a wolf age—
before the world goes headlong.
No man will have
mercy on another.

The power of the gods' weapons would lead the world and all its cities and castles to be consumed by fire.

Emil Doepler: The fiery stage of Ragnarök

Public domain image via Wikimedia Commons (ca. 1905)

Paradoxically, around the same time, there will be a terrible winter called Fimbulvetr or Fimbulwinter lasting for three years, and famine:

Black become the sun's beams
in the summers that follow,
weathers all treacherous.
Do you still seek to know? And what?

Sea levels also rise and flood the land.

In German, the concept of Ragnarök is called Götterdämmerung, which means Twilight of the Gods.

Carving on the stave church at Urnes, on an arm of Norway's Sognefjord, said to depict writhing serpents and dragons all biting each other in mutual destruction at Ragnarök

It takes a moment or two to work out the details. One of the dragons is a deer-like figure with spirals on its shoulders and haunches, and it is biting another dragon which is biting it in return.

Public domain image by Micha L. Rieser, via Wikimedia Commons

Lif (or Liv) and Lifthrasir, by Lorenz Frohlich, published 1895 in Karl Gjellerup, Den ældre Eddas Gedesange, *page 45*

Wikimedia Commons public domain artwork image

In the end, there are only two human survivors who, like Adam and Eve, gradually repopulate the world. These are Líf (the new Adam) and Lífthrasir (the new Eve), who survive the terrible turn of events by hiding in a forest called Hoddmímis Holt, which does not burn down in the fiery stages of the end of the world and is temperate enough to survive the great winter as well.

While to us this looks like a prophecy of some of the most serious dangers of our time, such as climate change and nuclear war, it's thought that in the time of the Vikings, tales like this were actually inspired by a mixture of the Vikings' concern at their own violent predilections, the general environmental precarity of the northern realm they inhabited, tales of the biblical Flood or something like it (which are culturally widespread), and the still-recent fact of the fall of the Western Roman Empire, a traumatic event which was made worse by sharp climatic deterioration in the 500s CE (the possible inspiration for Fimbulwinter): a decline and fall captured in the Anglo-Saxon poem *The Ruin* which describes sophisticated Roman architecture now abandoned to decay, most probably at Bath in England:

So, Ragnarök's not really a prophecy at all. It's just a moral story based on events that had already happened, like many other Viking tales.

Well, let's hope so, anyway.

Reference

The quotations in this chapter are from Ursula Dronke (trans.) *The Poetic Edda: Volume II: Mythological Poems,* Oxford University Press, 1997, ISBN 0-19-811181-9, as reproduced on Wikipedia, URL en.wikipedia.org/wiki/Ragnarök, accessed 21 October 2021, at pp 19 and 18 of the original work respectively.

For more, see:

a-maverick.com/blog/ twilight-of-the-gods-fire-and-ice

Conclusion

I GREATLY enjoyed my travels through Iceland. I was amazed by the idea of people living on this volcanic island, so close to the Arctic Circle.

But perhaps the most amazing thing was how it was that the descendants of the Vikings, possibly one of the more unpleasant cultures in history – though again perhaps we were all pretty unpleasant a thousand years ago – should have somehow transmuted into the modern Scandinavians and Icelanders, who have such a reputation for being moderate and sensible.

This shows how mutable the world is, and how changeable and 'fixable' things are where there's a will. Perhaps there are implications here for peacemaking: for everyone to stop mentally inhabiting the world of old-time Vikings and to think more like the modern Scandinavians and Icelanders. After all, it's a transition that's been made before.

Acknowledgements and Thanks

THANKS to everyone who helped me to discover Iceland.

Additional thanks are due to my editor Chris Harris, and to everyone who checked my manuscript along the way. As always, all errors and omissions that may remain are mine.

And thank you all once again, for reading and listening to my tale.

Other books by Mary Jane Walker

Did you like *Incredible Iceland?* If so, please leave a review!

And you may also like to have a look at the other books I've written, all of which have sales links on my website a-maverick.com.

A Maverick Traveller

A funny, interesting compilation of Mary Jane's adventures. Starting from her beginnings in travel it follows her through a life filled with exploration of cultures, mountains, histories and more.

A Maverick New Zealand Way

The forerunner of the present book, *A Maverick New Zealand Way* was a finalist in Travel at the International Book Awards, 2018.

A Maverick Cuban Way

Trek with Mary Jane to Fidel's revolutionary hideout in the Sierra Maestra. See where the world nearly ended and the Bay of Pigs and have coffee looking at the American Guantánamo Base, all the while doing a salsa to the Buena Vista Social Club.

A Maverick Pilgrim Way

Pilgrim trails are not just for the religious! Follow the winding ancient roads of pilgrims across the continent of Europe and the Mediterranean.

A Maverick USA Way

Mary Jane took Amtrak trains around America and visited Glacier, Yellowstone, Grand Teton, Rocky Mountain and Yosemite National Parks before the snow hit. She loved Detroit which is going back to being a park, and Galveston and Birmingham, Alabama.

A Maverick Himalayan Way

Mary Jane walked for ninety days and nights throughout the Himalayan region and Nepal, a part of the world loaded with adventures and discoveries of culture, the people, their religions and the beautiful landscapes.

A Maverick Inuit Way and the Vikings

Mary Jane's adventures in the Arctic take her dog sledding in Greenland, exploring glaciers and icebergs in Iceland, and meeting some interesting locals.

Iran: Make Love not War

Iran is not what you think. It's diverse, culturally rich, and women have more freedoms than you would imagine.

The Scottish Isles: Shetlands, Orkneys and Hebrides (Part 1)

In 2018, Mary Jane decided to tour the islands that lie off the coast of Scotland. She made it around the Orkney and Shetland groups, and to the inner-Hebrides islands of Raasay, Mull, Iona and Staffa as well. She was amazed to discover that Norse influences were as strong as Gaelic ones, indeed stronger on the Orkneys and Shetlands.

Catchy Cyprus: Once was the Island of Love

This is a short book based on Mary Jane's visit to Cyprus, the island that copper's named after and the legendary birthplace of Aphrodite, Greek goddess of love. A former British possession in the Mediterranean Sea, Cyprus is divided into Greek-dominated and Turkish-dominated regions with United Nations troops in between.

Lovely Lebanon: A Little Country with a Big History

"I visit the small country of Lebanon, north of Israel, a country whose name means 'the white' in Arabic because of its snow-capped mountains. Lebanon is divided between Christian and Muslim communities and has a history of civil war and invasion. For all that, it is very historic, with lots of character packed into a small space."

Eternal Egypt: My Encounter with an Ancient Land

In this book, Mary Jane explores Egypt, a cradle of civilisation described by the ancient Greek historian Herodotus as the 'gift of the Nile'. Mary Jane put off going to Egypt for years before she finally went. She's glad she did: there's so much more to Egypt than the pyramids!

The Neglected North Island: New Zealand's other half

In this book Mary Jane explores New Zealand's less touristy North Island. *The Neglected North Island* was judged **'Best Antipodean Cultural Travel Book 2021' by *Lux Life* magazine** (lux-review.com) and is also a **2021 IPPY Awards Bronze medallist** in Australia/New Zealand/Pacific Rim – Best Regional Non-Fiction

The Sensational South Island: New Zealand's Mountain Land

In this book, which is the companion to *The Neglected North Island,* Mary Jane explores New Zealand's mountainous South Island. She branches out from obvious tourist traps like Queenstown to explore this large but thinly populated island's lesser-known byways, historic cities and diverse landscapes, which vary from subtropical jungles where the world's southernmost palm trees grow, to much chillier places that look like Iceland and Greenland and even like Mars.

A Nomad in Nepal

A Nomad in Nepal and the Lands Next Door updates Mary Jane's earlier book, *A Maverick Himalayan Way*. With links to blog posts containing colour photographs and videos, *A Nomad in Nepal and the Lands Next Door* describes Mary Jane's three trips, so far, to Nepal and the Himalayan region.

Delving deeply into Himalayan history, *A Nomad in Nepal* is also a mine of useful firsthand experience about guiding and trekking pitfalls and the politics of the region, all while describing epic treks in Nepal and visits to Sikkim, Dharamshala (Himachal Pradesh), Sringagar (Kashmir) and the exotic Chitral region of Pakistan as well, hard-up against Afghanistan, where the local Kalash tribe is menaced by the Taliban.

A Kiwi on the Amtrak Tracks

Kiwi adventurer Mary Jane Walker explored America by Amtrak Train, travelling one and a half times around the lower 48 states and stopping off in Hawai'i as well. *A Kiwi on the Amtrak Tracks* is the latest book by the author of the IPPY award-winning *The Neglected North Island: New Zealand's other half* and award finalists *A Maverick New Zealand Way* and *Iran: Make Love Not War.*

Go Greenland

This short book, with photographs and links to blogs with more pictures, describes my adventures in Greenland, the great frozen but melting island east of Canada. Not all of Greenland is frozen, though, and some of it is green.

I travel from the southern tip of the island, where conditions are fairly mild and where there used to be a Viking colony, to the frozen Ilulissat Icefjord north of the Arctic Circle, where I go dog-sledding before it melts. As recently as 1850 the icefjord held a permanent glacier, the Jakobshavn Glacier, which has now almost disappeared.

Made in United States
Orlando, FL
07 September 2022

22143330R00098